KOURTNEY KING

Marriage Made Simple

The Emancipated Relationship: A Manual for Learning Marriage From The Mind of God

First published by The Emancipation Center Publishing 2026

First edition

This book was professionally typeset on Reedsy.
Find out more at reedsy.com

To every soul that has silently wondered if there was more to companionship.

Contents

Preface

The Shelter

I lived in a two-parent home until age nine. I was happy there. My mother made our home beautiful, almost dreamlike. We danced on the bed, singing loudly to Greek music. Sometimes we painted or baked. Other times, we designed or sewed. Occasionally, we played piano. My childhood overflowed with delight. I loved dressing in my mother's clothes and makeup, pretending to be her. She seemed regal to me. Wearing her things felt like stepping into her grace and adulthood, if only for a moment. When my father traveled, my mother let us climb into his big Ford truck. My brother steered, I pressed the pedals, and we laughed at our daring. She created a space where our imaginations could live.

My father was a disciplinarian when needed. He also brought us into his world. Wherever we went, he treated no one as a stranger. That filled me with wonder. His truck, which I named Truck, became a castle of laughter. His silly jokes and playful humor brightened every drive. Sometimes, we rode four-wheelers. Red dirt would swirl into the Oklahoma air. I held onto him and my brother in sheer joy. Occasionally, I helped him fix our cars. Not for the work, but to stay close to him. When he cooked, he seemed magical. He could turn random fridge ingredients into comforting meals. He brought energy and fun to our lives.

My life felt stable and safe. I went to school, church, my mother's clothing store, my grandparents', or a cousin's. Creativity filled our walls. Laughter echoed down the halls. Love lived in our home. But that stability would soon be disrupted, changing everything.

The Seed

Early one morning, my parents called my brother and me into their bedroom. The air felt different. Tense. My body tightened. We climbed into their waterbed, the four of us under a thick, bright-blue blanket my father brought back from one of his military trips to Hawaii. Beneath that weight and brightness, they told us they loved us but were no longer happy together. We would now have two homes.

The waterbed rocked beneath me. The blanket's weight pressed down. I felt I might sink. My parents' voices faded. A deep fear settled in. I sensed my happy world slipping away, replaced by uncertainty. I felt powerless.

At nine, I had no words for what I felt. Suddenly, home felt unsafe. Fear, exposure, sickness, and vulnerability overwhelmed me. In that moment, I lost my first love: my family.

From that day on, an undercurrent of awareness stayed with me. Love and happiness, I realized, could disappear without warning. As time passed, instability, disappointment, and emotional danger became associated with marriage. After my parents' separation, I observed pain and conflict. I couldn't understand them. By my teens, I had decided that marriage wasn't for me. Still, I grew up in a faith community. I heard that marriage was essential to adulthood and faith. That tension between past experiences and present expectations shaped my later choices.

The Search

At nine, I could not have known I would spend decades seeking safety in relationships. As I grew, I searched for someone to restore what I had lost. Seeking to be chosen put my happiness in others' hands. For years, I believed a man could heal my trauma, ease my insecurities, and prove my worth.

I married. I divorced. I dated. Each time, I quietly hoped someone would restore the stability I had lost under that heavy blue blanket.

Everything changed in adulthood when I learned what I am about to share. I gained a different understanding of companionship and a precise grasp of its mechanics. That insight gave me peace. Looking back, I wondered whether this knowledge could have helped my parents notice that love was unraveling right before their eyes.

It could have.

With my current understanding, I found strength, not in being chosen. I found contentment, not in relying on another to repair childhood wounds. I was no longer searching from a place of lack. I discovered the search itself had been unnecessary.

Today, I view companionship and marriage through their original design. I no longer seek someone to complete me or to restore what I lost that day. Now, I approach marriage and companionship with peace and logic.

The Shift

What changed was not my emotions, but my reference point.

I realized instability in relationships was not random. Without knowing it, I had been placing my security and happiness entirely in other people's hands. That pattern felt normal to me, even responsible and loving, but it was quietly driving everything.

When my reference point shifted, my logic about relationships shifted too. I stopped measuring my worth by who chose me or who stayed. I began living without fear, dependency, or the constant need for validation.

I learned a design that traces companionship to its original order, one older than my experiences and deeper than my disappointments. Seeing marriage through that lens, I realized its true purpose was never to fix a person's insecurities or fill what childhood left empty. It was something steadier than that. That is what this book is about. And it is what finally gave me peace.

Introduction

From the moment we are old enough to dream, we are told powerful stories about love and marriage. Films, novels, family traditions, religious lessons, and now an endless stream of online opinions shape our beliefs. Some see marriage as passion, others as safety, status, duty, or approval. Some still cling to the fairy-tale ending. But reality rarely matches those dreams. Relationships may start with excitement and hope. Over time, stress, distrust, and disappointment creep in. Many are left asking, "What went wrong?" The honest answer is that they were building on the wrong foundation from the beginning.

Even as these ideals persist, relationships still break down. Divorce rates climb. Families divide. Men and women suffer, and sometimes the damage is irreversible. Yet people keep recycling the same ideas, as if repetition makes them true. It takes courage to pause and ask: is this actually working? If the fruit keeps dying, the root is not healthy.

Most blame failed relationships on lost feelings or unmet expectations, but these are just symptoms. The deeper issue is relying on weak ideas that cannot support life. They see the fruit but never address the root.

What most people are never taught are the spiritual laws behind their relationships. A spiritual law is an invisible, unchanging principle that governs life. Like gravity, it operates whether a person understands it or not, and ignoring it does not make it stop working.

To see marriage clearly, we must see it as a system governed by spiritual laws. When marriage is based on feelings or a checklist, those things become its measure of success. It will eventually fail by that same measure. Marriage must follow life's rules, or it will not last. To operate effectively within any system, you must first understand its design.

This book offers something different. Rather than repeating the same ideas, it invites you out of ways of thinking that do not align with life's system. Marriage is treated here as more than romance, duty, or emotion. It is a living system, one that must be understood by its design. The goal is to give you a clear view of what marriage is, how it works, what distorts it, and how to bring your own marriage into alignment with that design.

I

Part 1: Foundations

What if everything you were taught about marriage was built on the wrong foundation?
This section begins at the beginning. Not with romance or tradition, but with design. Understanding what marriage is, at its core, changes how you see everything that comes after it.

1

Chapter 1: Marriage as a Living System

Conditional Illustration 1: The Silent House

Eve stared out the window. The Saturday morning sun was blinding. She did not notice.

She had been sitting at the kitchen table for twenty minutes with a cup of coffee she had not touched. The house was quiet. Not a comfortable quiet. An unsettling one. Adam was in the next room. That close. That far.

They had been married for four years.

She thought about their beautiful wedding. Her custom dress. The flowers. Her mother was crying in the front row. Her four closest friends were standing beside her in silk lavender.

Most of all, she thought of the way Adam looked at her when she walked down the aisle. Like she was the only person in the room. She had believed in that look. She had believed it meant something permanent, something that would keep confirming itself the way it did in those early months when everything felt like proof that she had finally chosen right.

The feeling had changed. Not all at once. Slowly. The way a season turns before you notice it has.

She still believed she loved him. She just did not feel seen by him the way she used to. He did not ask about her anymore. She had tried to tell him once, carefully. He had listened. Then he went back to whatever sport he was playing on his phone. She had felt more alone after the conversation than before it. She stopped trying after that.

She told herself she was not asking for too much. She just wanted to feel like the marriage was giving her something back. Like she mattered inside of it. Like she was not just managing a household, a schedule, and a version of herself she no longer recognized.

She used to be so happy.

She sighed. Took a sip of her coffee and winced. It was cold.

She did not know what was wrong with them. She only knew that this was not what she had imagined. And she could not figure out why doing everything right still felt like not enough.

Adam was lying on his back in the bedroom, phone in his hand, not watching the Nets game that was playing on it.

He was watching the small crack near the ceiling light fixture. He had noticed it months ago. Kept meaning to fix it. Never did. He stared at it now, irritated by its presence.

The house was silent. And somehow that silence made the crack between them more visible than the one in the ceiling.

He had provided everything he knew how to provide. A good home. Faithfulness. He did not understand what else was being asked of him. And not understanding had started to feel like failure. No matter how much he gave, the measurement she was using was one he could never quite reach.

His home was supposed to be the one place he could rest. A place where someone made him feel like his efforts meant something.

He had not said that to Eve because he did not have the words for it. He only knew that he was tired of how things had been.

He was frustrated. And tired of pretending he was not.

He set the phone down on his chest and closed his eyes. They needed to figure this out.

* * *

The Framework You Never Chose

What Eve and Adam were experiencing was not unique to them. It is happening in kitchens and bedrooms all over the world, in every culture, in every language, among people who love each other and cannot understand why that love is not enough to make the marriage work.

The problem is not the love. The problem is what they were taught about marriage.

Most people never choose a marriage framework. They inherit one. The way you inherit a language, a last name, or a set of beliefs about what a good life looks like. It is handed to them by their culture, their family, their religion, or the media. They carry it into the marriage without ever examining it, without ever asking whether it was designed to produce what they are hoping for.

It was not.

Globally, marriage tends to follow one of two inherited models. Both are deeply embedded in culture. Both feel natural to the people operating from them. Both produce the same result. Eve and Adam sat that afternoon as two people who did everything right and still ended up exhausted, disconnected, and unable to name why.

This chapter introduces both models, where they come from, what they produce, and why neither of them is the Garden.

Two Models of Marriage

Globally, marriage tends to follow either a personal-fulfillment model or a family-and-community model. In the personal-fulfillment model, marriage is often regarded as a response to loneliness and a source of meaning or identity. From early on, people are shaped by stories, media, and community standards to believe that finding the right partner ensures love, confirms self-worth, and completes their life. For many, marriage is a marker of stability, prestige, or achievement. Within this system, marriage is expected to address insecurity, support identity, and bring emotional satisfaction.

The family-and-community model regards marriage as a duty or collective obligation. It can function to keep order, preserve honor, and ensure continuity. Marriage, in this context, reaches beyond the couple. It involves fulfilling prescribed roles and meeting family or community expectations. Familial and social standards shape the meaning of marriage.

One model expects marriage to fulfill deep personal needs. The other expects it to satisfy family and community demands. Both treat marriage as a means to an end, with people hoping to gain love, worth, approval, or a sense of belonging. These competing demands are one reason many enter marriage sincerely, yet still encounter conflict, exhaustion, and discontent. Neither model addresses what actually sustains a marriage. Rather than centering on attraction, emotion, or tradition, this chapter considers marriage as a system regulated by spiritual laws and the unseen realities that shape it.

Spiritual Laws

A spiritual law is an unseen, immutable principle. It governs existence the way gravity governs how we move. Spiritual laws do not simply coexist with the physical world. They direct it. The physical world replicates the spiritual realm. Picture a concealed crack in a home's foundation. Sooner or later, that crack becomes a break in the wall. When a spiritual law is violated, visible problems will surface in a marriage.

When the mind is not aligned with spiritual laws, it begins to rely on external reference points. When external factors become the source, a person's perceptions and decisions become distorted. Over time, that distortion damages both the individual and the marriage.

A Manual for How Life Works

If spiritual laws govern life, then a source is required that reveals what those laws are and how they work. While many view the Bible as a religious rulebook, a history book, a devotional guide, or a list of moral ideas, this book approaches it in a different way. Here, the Bible is considered a manual for the mechanics of life, much as a car mechanic's manual explains how an engine works. Most people are unaware that the Scriptures contain patterns that reveal the laws and mechanics governing life and marriage. These laws originate from the Author of Life and apply regardless of people's awareness.

To use the spiritual laws found in the Bible as a manual for how to live life is an approach I call Applied Life Logic. This method interprets spiritual laws as universal mechanics rather than religious beliefs and relies on these principles to guide life and marriage. Many live in dysfunction because they respond to shifting external conditions and inherited opinions rather than unchanging laws. Applied Life Logic is a system that works every time it is properly applied.

This approach is not about faith as commonly defined; it addresses mechanics. Following the mechanics of how life was designed delivers peace and health as a matter of logical certainty. Just as engineers rely on the laws of physics for the safety of a bridge, the focus here is not to hope for a functional marriage, but to apply logic that produces one. When the desired result is missing, it means the underlying logic is not being properly applied.

To use the Bible in this way, treat it as an engineer or an electrician would treat a system. Study it deliberately to grasp how it functions and how it was intended to work. This book takes that analytical viewpoint, reading the Bible not for comfort, convention, moral counsel, or history, but as a manual revealing the mechanics of life. Many people read the Bible sincerely, but sincerity is not the same as knowing how to interpret a manual. Misinterpreting a manual can result in misuse or even abuse of what it was intended to guide.

Spiritual laws are fixed. They do not change because of emotion, opinion, or culture. Like gravity, they are unseen, but they still govern what happens in the visible world. When Scripture is read as a manual, it reveals how life actually works with that same consistency. This is why Hebrews 11:3 says that the worlds were framed by the word of God, and why 2 Corinthians 4:18 tells us not to focus only on what is seen, but also on what is unseen. Marriage is no different. What appears on the outside is being formed by something deeper. If the unseen logic is wrong, the marriage will eventually show it.

Since marriage produces results according to the unseen laws that govern it, the next question becomes: what exactly governs it? That question leads to the concept of a governing principle.

The Governing Principle

Relationships are the result of aligning with or departing from governing spiritual laws. Just as each person lives by a governing principle, so does a marriage. Every person enters a relationship with a reference point that shapes how they understand love, trust, conflict, safety, and intimacy. A reference point is the source a person uses to decide what is true, what matters, and who they are. It shapes how they interpret life, make decisions, and respond to what happens around them.

Your governing principle is your highest reference point. Whatever holds that place in you becomes the source of your logic, especially under pressure, conflict, or crisis. That is why Proverbs 4:23 says, "Keep thy heart with all diligence; for out of it are the issues of life." The outcomes in your marriage are not simply a matter of chance. They are flowing from the governing logic of the heart.

Because your reference point shapes how you understand relationships and what your life produces, it equally shapes the kind of relationship you establish. That reference point shapes every pattern and agreement within the marriage, whether healthy or unhealthy. What people often call compatibility, chemistry, shared values, family approval, or a sense of duty may be the visible result of a common reference point. That reference point is either rooted in spiritual laws or defined by outside influences.

Your reference point becomes the source of your logic. Logic is the inner system your mind uses to process reality, make decisions, and explain situations. It acts like an internal soundboard. Whatever a person uses as a reference point shapes how they think, reason, and respond. That logic shapes thoughts, emotions, and behavior. Behavior produces fruit. Marriage makes that whole process visible.

Because marriage makes one's governing principle visible, surface behavior is never the whole story. We must ask what source is producing that behavior.

Correcting the Source

Human behavior is the visible expression of a governing logic. Many people teach communication tools or conflict skills as the path to a healthy marriage. These tools might change how a person acts. However, they do not fix the problem at the source. Fixing a behavior is not the same as fixing the system. It is like a contractor trying to fix a collapsing building by repainting the walls while ignoring the damaged foundation. Because of this, many couples learn the language of a healthy marriage without ever experiencing marriage as it was originally designed.

A marriage reveals the logic of the people inside it. When a person's reference point depends on validation, reassurance, control, duty, family approval, social status, or inherited expectations, that dependency enters the marriage too.

Emotional security may become the spouse's responsibility. A facade of peace may be achieved only when everyone else is satisfied according to *their* respective reference points. This may result in exhaustion. Love may become mixed with control, fear, silent resentment, or the burden of always meeting expectations. When a marriage is held together this way, it is like a plumber patching a leak without fixing the broken pipe. Things may improve for a while, but the real problem remains.

If a person changes behavior without changing the reference point, that change will not last. It may look different for a time, but the same pattern will return because the source has not changed. A person can learn new words, better habits, and healthier responses and still feel strained, restless, and worn down. Lasting change requires more than behavior change. It requires a change in reference point.

If both the personal-fulfillment and the family-and-community models misplace responsibility in marriage, then a new perspective is needed. To find that, we must go back further than any cultural tradition. Back to where marriage actually began.

The Garden Model

Both models fall short for the same reason. Neither addresses what actually sustains a marriage. The answer is not found in a better version of either model. It is found in the original design.

In the Garden model, partnership is not established to fulfill romantic fantasy, social duty, or family expectations. It is established to cultivate, multiply, and steward life together from one foundation: the Spirit.

This is the missing link for Eve and Adam. Her unsettling loneliness and his silent frustration are the natural results of operating within inherited models that were never designed to produce what they were intended to. The solution is not for Adam to put down his phone or for Eve to ask for less. It is for both of them to return to the Garden.

This book uses the Garden model to emancipate marriages from misconceptions that were never part of God's original design. It points us back to the spiritual laws and principles He established from the beginning. This allows marriage to be understood, cultivated, and governed by the logic of the Spirit.

2

Chapter 2: Why This Framework Is Different

To move toward the Garden model and experience marriage as it was originally designed, we must first master the definitions that govern it. You cannot inhabit an environment if you do not speak its language or understand the laws that keep it standing. You may have already noticed that the way this book speaks about relationships and the Bible sounds different from what you are used to. That difference is not accidental. It is because of definitions.

A definition is a clear statement of what something is. It explains the meaning of a word or idea and helps distinguish it from other things. A definition also sets limits. It shows what belongs within a term and what does not. Without clear definitions, words may sound familiar while carrying very different meanings.

Definitions do three things: they set the boundary, program the logic, and produce the result. First, they show you what something is and what it is not. Second, they tell your mind how to think about that thing. Finally, they dictate how you act and respond to life. If your definitions come from external influences, you will begin to borrow your understanding from culture, emotions, family patterns, and the opinions of others. In that condition, you may be sincere, but the foundation will still be unstable.

Definitions are not just neutral language. They function as governing laws that frame your spirit and perception. The expectations they form will quietly shape every outcome in a relationship.

The Distinction of This Framework

At this point, something must be made clear. Familiar language does not mean identical meaning. Shared vocabulary does not mean shared logic. This distinction is worth holding onto, because it shapes everything that follows in this chapter.

Words such as love, peace, wisdom, covenant, order, submission, trust, sex, and freedom may appear in philosophy, psychology, physiology, religion, and popular culture. That does not mean those systems are saying the same thing as this framework. In fact, to state it plainly, they are not.

This framework uses Applied Life Logic to bypass opinion. While psychology observes behavior, Applied Life Logic analyzes the functional mechanics of the spirit. We are not looking for "tips" to make you feel better. We are using the precise logic that allows the system to run without internal resistance. By applying this logic, we move from the abstract "hope" of other models to a governing certainty of the Spirit.

The Garden model is the blueprint. It is the original design for how marriage was presented in the Garden. Applied Life Logic is the technical process used to apply that model to your marriage and your life. One is the target. The other is the science required to reach it.

The Garden model of marriage is not philosophy because it is not rooted in human ideas created apart from the Spirit to explain life. It is grounded in spiritual laws and principles that govern how life actually works. Philosophy becomes abstract when it relies on human conclusions, feelings, and theories rather than on living laws that consistently produce the same result.

The Garden model is different. It concerns itself with functioning from the Spirit in all of humanity, and what actually produces life, order, and peace in human relationships from it.

It is not physiology because it is not built on hormones, nervous system states, or bodily reactions as final authorities. Those things may help explain what the body is doing, but they do not tell us what governing source produced it.

It is not psychology because it is not built on behavior as the final point of interpretation. Psychology may describe what a person does, but observation alone does not reveal or correct the source from which that behavior flows.

It is not built on pop culture or inherited culture. The Garden model does not treat emotional intensity, attraction, familiarity, or self-expression as final authorities.

It is also not built on inherited roles, family pressure, communal expectations, or social order as final authorities. Those things may shape how marriage is practiced in a community, but they do not define God's original design for it.

It is not a religion built on moral performance, social conformity, or behavior management. The concern here is the source of logic, function, and the restoration of the original design first established in mankind.

Because this framework is distinct, its definitions must remain distinct as well. Therefore, the definitions are self-existent in themselves. This means they are independent and do not require external validation to function. They are fixed, original standards that exist on their own authority. They do not bend to fit your experience; your experience must be brought into alignment with them.

The Danger of Mixed Definitions

To mix anything with the Garden Model does not enrich the framework. It contaminates it. When readers import outside definitions into a self-existent system simply because the words sound familiar, they alter what is being presented. They may still use the same vocabulary, but the logic underneath has shifted.

The danger here is conceptual distortion from borrowed definitions. External systems, specifically religious ones, have taken words like covenant, submission, and love and redefined them through the lens of control, tradition, or performance. When you bring these borrowed definitions into the Garden, you introduce a virus that disrupts the internal governance of your home. You must factory reset your vocabulary using the manual's original definitions before the system can function. Precision matters because you cannot establish a life on terms you do not accurately define.

This is how confusion enters. A person may hear the word 'love' and silently define it as romance. They may hear submission and define it through domination. They may hear peace and define it as silence. They may hear intimacy and define it through attachment. When this happens, the framework is no longer being understood on its own terms. It is being blended with foreign definitions, and what it can produce becomes distorted.

This is why precision matters so deeply in this book. I am not asking the reader to compare this framework casually with every familiar system and assume they all mean the same thing. I am asking the reader to let this framework define itself from within, according to its own laws, terms, and structure. Only then can it be understood accurately. Only then can it function properly. Because this framework is different, it also requires a different way of reading Scripture.

The Bible as a Technical Manual

This background matters because this book is not asking you to read Scripture as a collection of moral sayings or inspiring stories. It asks you to read Scripture as a technical and cognitive manual that explains how the human spirit works.

A technical manual explains how something is designed to function. A cognitive manual shows how thought, understanding, judgment, and response are meant to work. Together, they frame how Scripture is read here: as a guide to how humanity is meant to operate from the Spirit outward.

Biblical principles can be understood in a similar way to the laws of physics. Just as invisible laws such as gravity consistently govern the physical world, Scripture reveals invisible laws that govern human outcomes. These laws do not change with emotion, opinion, or culture. They remain fixed. For this book, I will not teach the technical process of reading Scripture. That is a study in itself. What matters here is understanding that this book is reading Scripture as a manual of function, and that approach shapes every definition that follows.

Once this is understood, the importance of definitions becomes impossible to ignore. Definitions are never neutral. They install the governing logic a person uses to interpret reality. Proverbs 4:7 says, "Wisdom is the principal thing; therefore get wisdom: and with all thy getting get understanding." Understanding is the precision of your definitions. To understand a thing is not simply to recognize its name. It is to know its true nature, its limits, and its function accurately enough to operate with it the right way.

These two concepts are worth pausing on, because everything that follows in this book depends on them. A technical manual explains how something works, what governs its operation, and what causes it to function well or break down. A cognitive manual explains how the mind is meant to work, including its logic, definitions, and thought patterns that shape how a person sees and responds to life. Simply put, Scripture is a manual that tells us how something functions. It reveals God's governing logic and the order by which life is meant to operate. That matters because the definitions a person accepts will shape the logic they use, and that logic will shape how they interpret, establish, and live.

Why the Bible Can Be Trusted

Scripture can be trusted because it begins with God, not with broken man trying to understand life from below. God is consistent, self-existent, and unchanging. Because the Bible begins with Him, it stands on a firm foundation and gives life meaning. It does not shift with feelings, trends, pain, or public opinion. It begins with the highest truth. This is what makes Scripture different. It does not only deal with outward behavior or visible problems. It deals with causes. It goes to what is ruling the heart, the mind, the tongue, and the direction of a person's life.

The Bible can be trusted because it is a decodable system of spiritual laws. Through Applied Life Logic, we stop treating the text as a collection of historical stories and start treating it as the source code for functionality. When you decode the pattern, the authority is not found in religious tradition; it lies in the law revealed by the text. This code remains consistent and produces a predictable outcome every time it is correctly applied.

The Bible is practical because it not only talks about invisible things. It speaks to thought, identity, judgment, action, and result. It shows how life is meant to be ordered. It does not just help a person manage symptoms. It reveals the laws by which life is either built up or broken down. It shows what produces order and what produces disorder, what restores life and what breaks it apart. That is why it is practical. It reaches the place in a person where life is being governed. Because Scripture begins with God, God becomes the highest standard in the system. He is not just someone the Bible talks about. He is the One by whom life is to be understood.

That means Scripture teaches a person to define identity by what comes from God rather than by wounds, failure, labels, feelings, or public opinion. It teaches a person to judge life by God's nature and promises rather than by appearances alone. Because the Bible is the ultimate schematic, it trains a person to reason from truth rather than fear, from life rather than lack, and from covenant rather than reaction. It directs action by divine order rather than by impulse or pressure. It also teaches a person what to expect, because when life is ruled by God, it should produce order, fruitfulness, wisdom, restoration, strength, and life. That is why the Bible can be trusted. It not only describes what is broken, but also what is working. It shows the standard by which life is meant to function.

The Bible Has Been Altered

Some people argue that the Bible cannot be trusted because it has been translated many times, handled by men, and shaped by culture or human agendas. That concern makes sense, but it does not address the deeper point. The Bible does not have authority because every translator was perfect or because every culture handled it without error. It can still be trusted because its deeper order and meaning remain.

The Bible works like a law. A law does not stop being true just because someone explains it badly, misunderstands it, or uses it poorly. Gravity still works even when people do not fully understand it. Fire still burns according to its nature, even when people misuse it.

Think of it as a master architectural blueprint that has been photocopied and passed through the hands of hundreds of workers over many years. The paper may have coffee stains, some edges may be torn, and laborers may even have scribbled their own notes in the margins. However, the structural math required to keep the building standing is still encoded in those lines. No matter how messy the paper gets, the load-bearing requirements remain the same. An engineer who knows how to read the math can still build the skyscraper perfectly because the original intent is baked into the design.

In the same way, the spiritual laws, definitions, and patterns encoded in Scripture do not disappear just because people have handled the text imperfectly. People may cloud the surface, but they cannot remove the deeper order woven into it. This is why the Bible can still be trusted. Even where language has changed, and translation has limits, the deeper patterns remain. The links between ideas remain. The ruling principles remain. Human error cannot destroy the deeper structure of the text. That deeper structure is one reason Scripture still carries authority.

The Source

This framework is different, and that raises a fair question: where does it come from?

What I am presenting here did not come from my own ideas. I first encountered this framework through the International Institute of Pneumatology, where I was trained in applied pneumatology, the study of how the logic of the Spirit is applied in daily life. The Bible was taught there as a decodable system of spiritual laws and principles, and I applied that framework to my whole life and watched it produce real results. That is the foundation on which this book stands.

Assumptions in Marriage

People often enter companionship with strong feelings but different definitions. Definitions are like a blueprint. They tell you what something is, how it works, and what is being established. When definitions differ, it is like two contractors following two different blueprints on the same house. The structure will suffer because they are not working from the same plan.

A relationship without shared definitions is like building a house from two different blueprints. The marriage becomes shaped by hidden expectations, private assumptions, and unspoken demands. Once that happens, disappointment feels personal, even when the real problem was a lack of shared understanding. Amos 3:3 asks, "Can two walk together, except they be agreed?" When something has not been properly defined, each person assumes they understand the other. That private understanding then begins to govern the relationship.

This is the danger of borrowed definitions. Most couples use the same words, like love or support, while operating on completely different data gathered from the outside world. They are speaking the same language, but they are not operating on the same logic. This is why this chapter has focused so carefully on definitions. Before two people can establish a life together, they must share an understanding of what they are establishing.

If the meanings are distorted, the relationship will begin in confusion. But that is also where the hope begins. What has been unclear can be defined.

3

Chapter 3: The Garden Model of Marriage

The Garden of Eden was humanity's original environment. It was where humans first used their ability to think and reason in alignment with the Spirit of God. Here, God revealed His plan for marriage.

The First Law

The Garden was not just a beautiful park or a utopian experience. Instead, it was a place with structure, boundaries, and purpose. For life in the Garden to remain healthy, everything had to follow the laws God established.

The foundational spiritual law in the Garden of Eden was the Law of Reproduction: everything, seen and unseen, reproduces after its own kind. An apple tree produces apples. A lion produces lions. Nothing in the Garden produces what is not in its nature. This is an unbreakable principle.

This law is the foundation of self-existence: an identity and a life not dependent on anything external. God is the ultimate self-existent Spirit. He functions according to His own internal logic and does not rely on anything outside Himself to exist or find validation. Anything He reproduces is also self-existent. When God breathed His life into man, He was not making a weak or dependent creature. He was multiplying His own independent nature.

In the Garden, man possessed God's spiritual identity. He was able to govern his domain without relying on physical creation for wisdom or value. He did not seek external validation; his identity came directly from God. This made him an independent force, bringing life and order.

In the Garden, man and woman looked to God's wisdom for direction. Genesis 2:7 says God "breathed into his nostrils the breath of life; and man became a living soul." The Breath of Life gave them vision and showed them how to live. It was more than oxygen; it shaped their thoughts and choices. It gave them God's character. It formed their spiritual DNA, enabling them to live from God's Spirit.

Because they were self-existent, they were also self-determining, meant to reason and govern from the Spirit within. Their actions were not driven by inadequacy, insecurity, or external pressure.

The Garden model was unique because man and woman were joined by the Breath of Life, the wisdom of the Spirit. Since both were meant to live from the same Breath, the woman's formation should be viewed accordingly.

The Law of Shared Governance

To understand the woman is to understand that her formation and her function were one and the same. Once we recognize that she was built from the structural Spirit of the man, we must also recognize that she was built to share his jurisdiction.

Woman's Formation

Genesis 2:21–22 describes the woman being formed from the man's side. This was not a physical bone being removed from a skeleton. The word "rib" (tsela) actually referred to a side-structure or a supporting beam. The structure for all things is the Spirit of God. In the man in the Garden, this spiritual structure was the Breath of Life.

The Breath of Life was the spiritual material that gave him his authority, logic, and strength. To create woman, God did not return to dust. He put man to sleep, split the Spirit within him, and placed it in the woman.

By taking from man's side structure, God ensured that the woman was also an exact expression of Him. They were two forms from one Source. Genesis 2:23 records the man saying, "This is now bone of my bones, and flesh of my flesh," seeing the woman as a multiplication of his Source. Like the man, the woman's worth was anchored in the Spirit.

The Helper

When God stated it was "not good for man to be alone" in Genesis 2:18, it specifically meant that man should not be alone in his authority to govern and expand the Garden. He did not need a servant. He needed a second source of power to help cultivate and maintain the Garden.

Before woman was formed, man named all the animals. Animals could help physically, but not spiritually. Man needed a helper who matched his internal structure, one who stood in equity and shared his Spirit-source. No animal could offer that.

She was not made to be managed or serve a man's needs, but to partner in ruling. The woman was designed as a co-creator and fellow authority, sharing responsibility for dominion.

They were not two different kinds of beings. They were one kind of being standing in two different spots to ensure the Garden was managed from every side. Think of it like a pair of hands. Both hands, the left and the right, have the power to grip, write, and build. They are different only in their position, so that they can work together to hold what one hand cannot do alone.

Cultivating and Keeping

God's design for marriage carried responsibility. Genesis 2:15 says, "And the Lord God took the man, and put him into the garden of Eden to dress it and to keep it." This was more than gardening. It showed what humanity was meant to do with life. In marriage, the man and woman were meant to be keepers of life together.

To cultivate means to nurture life and serve it. It means taking responsibility for its growth. To keep means to guard, protect, and set boundaries against anything that would weaken or attack life. Cultivating and keeping show what man and woman were to do with the marriage God placed in their care. They were to nurture and protect it as they did the Garden.

As the Law of Reproduction dictates, you can only cultivate what you are. In a healthy garden, one tree does not consume the next to survive. It draws life from its own root, stands in its own strength, and produces fruit after its kind. Marriage was meant to work the same way. It was a place to cultivate life, multiply it, and keep it in order.

Marriage was not governed by personal need or outside pressure. It was governed by shared responsibility for the life two people were building together.

Becoming One and Sex

Becoming one must be understood correctly. Many believe sex makes two people one. But sex alone cannot establish a union.

In the Garden, becoming one started before sex. It began with having one mind. Sex is not the start of union; it is the body's expression of a deeper reality already present.

When two people do not live from the same source, sex does not solve that problem. It may create attachment, intensity, or a temporary sense of closeness. But it cannot establish the unity for which marriage was designed. A relationship can have sex and still be divided in vision and purpose.

In the Garden model, sex was not meant for validation, identity, easing insecurity, or holding a relationship together. It was to express a union that already existed in the mind. So, becoming one cannot be reduced to physical intimacy. It must first be a spiritual reality before it is expressed in the body.

Love as Equity

In the Garden model, love is fundamentally equity. It is not about emotional intensity or fulfilling needs. It is not about dominance or self-sacrifice for the sake of peace. Love operates through mutual dignity, care, and freedom.

Equity means giving the other person the same care, dignity, and freedom you also give yourself. You do not use your strength against them, nor do you ignore your own life to please them. You nurture life in both directions. Love in marriage must come from the Spirit, so it can protect life, honor truth, and allow both people to stay whole.

This kind of love is very different from other models of marriage. The personal-fulfillment model reduces love to an emotional need. The family-and-community-governed model reduces it to mere duty. The Garden model shows something else entirely: love as equity, the right administration of life between two people who are both meant to live from the Spirit. That distinction matters because the model you use will determine how you love.

Marriage in the Garden was not rooted in need, emotion, or social expectation. It was rooted in shared source, shared governance, and shared responsibility for life. That is the standard. Everything that distorts marriage distorts one or more of those three things. The next chapter examines where that distortion begins.

4

Chapter 4: The Conditional Mindset

Mankind lost its original reference point in the Garden of Eden. Instead of living from the Spirit within, they chose another source of wisdom. Genesis 2:7 shows man first lived by the Breath of Life. In Genesis 3, that changed.

Man was designed to live from the self-existent Spirit. But when he listened to the serpent, his attention shifted to the tree of the knowledge of good and evil. Three things then took place in Adam's mind.

First, Adam used something outside himself to define who he was. By looking to the physical tree for wisdom, he abandoned his self-existent spiritual identity and role as Governor of Creation and let the tree become his reference point.

Second, Adam measured what he lacked by comparing himself to the physical creation. Because the tree had leaves and he did not, he reasoned he was naked and inadequate. He used something physical to measure his worth instead of something spiritual.

Third, Adam looked for validation. Because he felt exposed and ashamed, he sewed fig leaves together to cover what he believed was lacking. He tried to validate himself and hide his shame according to his new external logic. Genesis 3:5-7 and Genesis 3:10 show this.

That single decision changed everything. Where man had once been Spirit, light, and self-existent life, he was now dust, darkness, and death.

They were meant to live from the Spirit and govern creation, not use creation to define themselves. By giving more weight to what was visible than to the Spirit within, everything changed.

Their identity changed. Instead of functioning as self-existent beings, they began to function as adam, which means dust.

Their definitions changed. They began defining themselves and their reality in terms of physical measurements rather than by the Spirit.

Their logic and spiritual laws changed. They shifted from cultivating life with spiritual law to following the external law of comparison, reaction, and acquisition.

Their species changed. They went from being a species that functioned in light to a species that functioned in darkness.

Their relationship with creation changed. Instead of effortlessly governing the earth, they toiled, sweated, and controlled it by force.

Their relationship with one another changed. Instead of operating as self-existent beings in peace and equity, they began to function as codependent partners using demand, control, and pressure.

Their relationship with God changed. Instead of living in continuous union with and validation from the Spirit within, they saw God as a distant, external authority they had to appease.

This shift did not stop with individual experience. The new reference point led humanity to create systems outside of the Spirit. People needed new ways to explain God, define success, define marriage, define themselves, and seek validation.

Adam and Eve had no external religion. What they had was internal. Their doctrine, their rituals, and their understanding of God and governance were all written in their spirit. Religion, in every form, is a product of the conditional mindset. When man lost the Spirit as his internal reference point, he began building external systems to explain, reach, or appease a God who now felt distant and external. Religion is not the restoration of the original order. It is evidence that the original order was lost.

The Conditional Mindset

That decision formed what I call the Conditional Mindset. It creates a way of living in which external conditions determine a person's stability. Things outside of them begin to shape their identity. Whether life goes the way they want determines their peace of mind. Others' approval, their performance, and their ability to stay in control shape their confidence. Even when they do not realize it, these things make their emotions rise and fall.

Once the Spirit no longer ruled within, human beings began building life from the outside in.

This is why validation becomes so important in the conditional world. People do not seek it because they are shallow. They seek it because life's structure has changed. When external conditions rule a person, the world around them shapes their perspective and experience. People become reactive instead of settled. As Proverbs 25:28 warns, "He that hath no rule over his own spirit is like a city that is broken down, and without walls." Without a governing principle based on the Spirit within, the soul opens itself to whatever comes from outside.

This shift did not remain private. It spread into relationships and changed how companionship functioned.

What governs a person inwardly shapes how they love, speak, expect, respond, and relate. When the Conditional Mindset governs the mind, it enters the relationship and shapes how marriage functions.

The Conditional Marriage

When the Conditional Mindset rules, it shapes the marriage into a Conditional Marriage. Spouses use one another for emotional validation, reassurance, stability, or resources. The relationship feels transactional. Each measures what they give and what they expect in return.

A husband may provide financial security and then expect submission, peace, or agreement in return. A wife may offer affection, emotional support, sex, or care and then expect constant affirmation, attention, and proof of love in return. One spouse may think, "If I am doing all of this for you, then you should respond the way I want." The other may think, "If I am giving you this much of myself, then I should never have to wonder how you feel about me."

In this kind of marriage, a delayed text can feel like rejection. A different opinion can make you perceive disloyalty. Silence makes you assume something is wrong by default. Because a person ties their worth to these external conditions, the marriage fills with unspoken expectations, quiet demands, disappointment, and resentment. One person may feel used, while the other may feel unseen. Both can feel exhausted.

What was designed to be an environment of peace becomes a battlefield of unmet expectations.

A marriage built on the Conditional Mindset cannot produce lasting peace. While it may include moments of affection, effort, and sincerity, external conditions still rule it rather than the Spirit.

This is why restoration is needed. Not a better communication strategy or a new set of rules, but a change in the governing reference point itself. Until the Spirit rules within, the Conditional Mindset will continue to shape the marriage. The next chapter examines what that restoration requires.

* * *

Conditional Illustration 2: The Transaction

Eve's phone buzzed on the nightstand.

Her mother had already called twice that day. Eve had let both calls go to voicemail.

She grabbed the phone reluctantly.

"Hey, Mom."

Her mother did not waste time. "You just have to stop being so sensitive. Adam is a good man. He provides. He comes home every night. Do you know how many women would give anything for what you have?"

Eve sat on the bed.

"I know he's a good man, Mom." She whispered exhaustedly into the phone.

"From where I am standing, you have everything. A man who works, who stays, who does not run around. And you are sitting there unhappy like a lost puppy. That is not Adam's problem, Eve. That is yours."

Eve said nothing. Her chest tightened. She closed her eyes.

Her mother's voice softened. "I love you, Evie. You know I do. But you have always been too much in your feelings. Adam is not a feelings man. He is a doing man. You have to appreciate what he does instead of always needing something more from him."

Her mother had been married three times. She was now on her third husband, a quiet, sweet British man named Nigel. Her mother was happy to be married. Happy to be a kept woman. Being married was her goal. To her, being married meant you had done something right. What happened inside the marriage was a separate matter. Something you managed privately. Something you did not complain about too loudly. And Adam, in her mother's eyes, was everything a husband should be. Steady. Responsible. Faithful. So, the fact that Eve was unhappy was not a reflection of the marriage. It was a reflection of Eve.

Eve would not dare mention that Adam had not yet made it home and that it was after 7 o'clock. She would not dare mention the roses he had brought home yesterday, or that she had tried to be intimate with him, or that she had not enjoyed it. Her mother would blame her for it all.

And maybe she was to blame.

After she hung up, she sat on the edge of the bed. She cried. Silently.

She had heard it her whole life. You are too sensitive. You want too much. Appreciate what you have. She had tried. But the trying had made her feel hollow. And she did not know how much longer she could live in a quiet house with a man her mother adored and still feel completely alone.

Do I even still love my husband?

Adam walked into the house, exhausted from an extended meeting at work, and overheard Eve on the phone.

The tension in her voice let him know she was speaking with her mother.

He no longer said anything about it. He felt it every time. And he dreaded how Eve would look at him after their conversations. Like she was trying to reconcile the man her mother saw and the man she actually lived with.

He liked her mother. She understood him and appreciated what he did. He just wished Eve could do the same.

He was not angry at her. He did not fully understand what he was feeling. He only knew that somewhere along the way, Eve had started to feel more like a housemate than a wife.

The discomfort at home made work his safe space. He worked with some decent people. Sometimes he and Drew, in finance, played basketball in the corporate gym. Drew lost every game, but loved to play.

His coworker, Delilah, had an office that was not too far from his. She always seemed to notice things Eve no longer did. She asked about his weekend as if she was genuinely interested. She was always the first to notice his haircut. She always grabbed him a cup of coffee when she got one for herself. Small things. Meaningless things.

Yesterday, Delilah had asked how Eve had been. He had said she was fine. She had looked at him like she could tell he was not telling the truth. Then, as she left for the day, she stopped at his door. "Get her some flowers, Adam," she said. "There is a shop on 37th, just off Fifth. Beautiful arrangements." She had smiled and kept walking.

On his way home, he stopped at the shop and bought a dozen red roses. When he got home, he set them on the counter and kissed her cheek. Eve had smiled, said thank you, and put them in the cerulean blue crystal vase he had given her for their last anniversary.

The roses had done something. That night, she had reached for him instead of the other way around. He had felt, briefly, like his wife was back. She had been his, at least in body. But her mind was somewhere else entirely.

He was *not* interested in Delilah. Or any other woman. He was not that kind of man. But he noticed that he felt more seen in a few minutes of casual conversation with Delilah than he had felt in almost two years inside his own marriage.

That bothered him more than he wanted to admit.

He was not looking for anything outside of his marriage. He just wanted his marriage to be a marriage again.

He heard Eve end the conversation with her mother. The house returned to silence.

5

Chapter 5: The Restoration of Image

The decision described in the chapter on the Garden not only affected the man and the woman who made it. It affected every human being who came after them. It set in motion a corruption that no human effort could reverse. That is why restoration had to come entirely from outside the corrupted order.

In Genesis 3, God declared that the seed of the woman would bruise the serpent's head, and the serpent would bruise His heel. This was the first promise of restoration. It showed that God already intended to restore the Spirit, the mankind, and the earth to their original order. It also pointed forward to Jesus Christ, or Yeshua in Hebrew, who would bring the mindset of death and codependency under judgment and destroy its rule.

The Work of Christ

Christ has often been reduced to a historical person or a religious figure. But what happened through Him was not a religious event.

The Executive Mandate

The prophet Isaiah declared that "the government shall be upon His shoulder." This was not a prediction of a new religion, but a declaration of a new administration. In our modern world, we think of government as a building or a political party, but in the original order, government is simply the exercise of authority and the maintenance of order. When the first man shifted his reference point, he abandoned the government of the Spirit for a government of the self. Christ came to shoulder the responsibility of that failed administration. He did not come to lobby for a better moral code; He came as a King to physically and legally repossess the species and the territory. It was a governing shift in the order of the human species, as precise and irreversible as a law of physics.

When humanity shifted its reference point and lost its governing source, Christ stepped in to reverse that order entirely. He took the corrupted and codependent nature of the dust species, nailed that corrupted spirit to the cross, and breathed it out completely. By rising from the dead and stepping into a physical garden, He restored the original Garden of Eden order to the human spirit.

His suffering was not meaningless. It was the full confrontation of the corrupted condition that had ruled humanity. On the cross, He brought that governing order under judgment.

His burial marked the end of death and darkness's claim to rule.

His resurrection from the dead introduced a higher order of life. It was a Spirit stronger than death. His resurrection functioned with the consistency of a law of physics. Just as gravity operates on every person regardless of whether they understand it, the resurrection established a permanent governing reality. Anyone who aligns with it is brought under a new order of life.

His ascension repositioned the species. In the Garden, man had been given governing authority over all of creation. That authority was lost when the reference point shifted. When Yeshua ascended, He did not go alone. He carried the restored human species with Him into a position above every governing force in creation. This was not symbolic. It was a structural repositioning, like a law of physics restoring an object to its original orbit. Ephesians 2:6 states that those in Christ are seated with Him in heavenly places, above principalities, powers, and every name that is named.

Through the spiritual law of sowing and reaping, He sowed a perfect, uncorrupted life into the earth and reaped a new species. He did not patch the old order. He replaced it entirely.

How He Restored What Was Lost

First, He absorbed the corruption as His own.

When the first man fell, he gave the spirit of death and darkness authority over creation. Yeshua voluntarily stepped in and allowed that spirit of death to exhaust its full strength on His physical body when He was beaten. This can be seen in Isaiah 53:4–6, Romans 8:3, and 1 Peter 2:24.

Second, there was a legal reversal. Yeshua was completely innocent, but death still took His life. In doing this, death broke the spiritual law of equity and lost its right to rule. Yeshua nailed that corrupted, codependent human identity to the cross and breathed it out. In doing this, He brought the old dust species to an end. This can be seen in Acts 2:24, Romans 6:6, Luke 23:46, and Hebrews 2:14.

Third, there was the resurrection. When God raised Yeshua from the dead, He did it by a Spirit stronger than the first man and stronger than death itself. Because Yeshua is the head of the new human species, His resurrection became a spiritual law of life. Just as gravity pulls a dropped object to the ground, His resurrection has now pulled humanity into life with Him. This can be seen in Romans 1:4, Romans 6:9, 1 Corinthians 15:21–22, 1 Corinthians 15:45, and Colossians 1:18.

A Species Reality

Because this is a species issue, it transcends human belief systems. Gravity does not require your belief to function; it is a law of the environment. In the same way, the restoration Christ brought is a structural reality for the human race. You do not have to be religious to recognize that the human condition is currently functioning outside of its original design. Whether you are from the East or the West, whether you are a skeptic or a scholar, you are occupying a body that was designed for a specific governing Source. Aligning with Christ is not about joining a group; it is about a member of the species returning to the only Government capable of sustaining its life and authority.

Realignment

Realignment and restoration are for everyone, regardless of culture, religion, sex, or location. Christ does not belong to one race, one class, one nation, or one religious group. The restoration of the image of God is open to all. This is the heart of it: believing in Christ means believing that the image of God has been restored in you.

Everything else in this book flows from that one reality.

When you accept this governing reality, you are accepting that the Spirit that created you has been restored as the life within your spirit, soul, and body.

The Apostle Paul called this "Christ in you, the hope of glory" in Colossians 1:27. Glory means that position, authority, and light have been restored to you through Him and will be visibly seen by others.

Scripture also states, "If one died, all died." This means His death included *everyone* who identified with it. So do His resurrection and ascension. When He was crucified, the old version of you that lived from external reference points was terminated. This is what makes the next decision the most significant one a person can make:

Believing the truth about Christ is not a religious decision or a desperate plea to escape hell. It is a decision about who will be your source.

No matter your background, this heart vow is necessary for each person, because religion, family, relationships, and culture cannot make this vow for you. It is a real choice to change your spiritual identity and your reference point. It means turning away from living by external conditions and validation. It means receiving the self-existent Spirit of Christ as the life by which you now think and live.

The Two Actions of Realignment

This change involves two connected actions: believing in your heart and confessing with your mouth. Believing is the inward agreement to leave external validation behind and trust the Spirit of Christ in you as your *own* mind and life.

Confessing is the outward declaration of that agreement. In this framework, to confess does not simply mean admitting a historical fact or repeating words out loud. When Scripture speaks of confessing with your mouth, it means making a solemn, personal vow to take on the identity of the Spirit of Christ in you and to commit your life to living from that Spirit alone. From that point forward, the way you speak becomes evidence of the decision you made in your heart.

When you confess with your mouth, you are not merely repeating words; you are making a binding statement. By speaking from the Spirit, you are enforcing the laws of your new governing order. You are notifying every spiritual force that it no longer holds a legal claim on your time, your mind, your health, or your identity. Your voice is not a religious instrument. It is a governing one, backed by the highest Government in all of creation. You are using it to enforce the laws of your new Kingdom in the physical world.

When you make this agreement, a spiritual death and rebirth take place. What man was in the Garden (Spirit-sourced, self-existent, and governing) is what is being restored in you. You stop living by the world's conditions and begin living by the Spirit. You enter a new legal spiritual state: resurrected into a new, authorized Christ-species and legally relocated from the dominion of darkness into the light. You begin to govern your life by aligning your thoughts, imagination, and actions with His promises. A promise is everything God has declared you own when you make the decision to live from the Spirit of Christ within you.

This decision is more than a change in behavior; it is a total change of government. When you align with Christ, you are legally moving from one spiritual nation to another. You are renouncing your old citizenship in the kingdom of darkness and becoming a naturalized citizen of the Kingdom of

God. This is a legal transfer of authority. You are now governed by a different set of laws and a different King. As Colossians 1:13 says, "He has delivered us from the power of darkness and conveyed us into the kingdom of the Son of His love." You are a new species with a new territory, living under a new authority.

Baptism

This is where the significance of baptism comes into focus. Baptism is the physical act that mirrors this legal move. It is not a religious ritual or a simple tradition; it is your public oath of citizenship. By going under the water, you are performing a public renunciation of the old spiritual government. You are declaring to every governing force in the universe that your old, independent self is dead and has no more legal right to rule your life. You are effectively tearing up your old passport.

The word baptism means to be immersed. Just as a cloth takes on the color of the dye it is dipped in, you are being immersed in Christ to take on His nature. You are putting on His identity as your new operational self. It is your formal entrance into the resurrected species. You rise out of the water to function as a legal member of a new nation, no longer living as a diminished version of yourself, but as a restored member of the Christ-species with the authority to act on the King's behalf.

The Sealing of the Holy Spirit

Once the vow is made, you are sealed with the Holy Spirit, who becomes your new governing intelligence. To be sealed means you are completely encompassed by the Spirit, the way liquid is held inside a bottle. You are entirely clothed in His presence. From that point, the Holy Spirit becomes your absolute reference point. You stop relying on external things, whether society, careers, or changing emotions, to validate your identity or direct your decisions. Your mind is now governed by the self-existent logic of the Spirit within you. You are now responsible for learning how to live from that Spirit.

Trusting in Christ means returning to the Spirit as your source. He did not restore humanity so people could stay trapped in the disorder that had taken hold of the species. He restored the image of God so the species could return to its original identity, source, and function.

Why Christ Came Through Israel

Some may ask why Christ came through Israel. To understand that, we have to go back to the beginning of the biblical story. In Scripture, two lines begin to appear. One came through Abel. After Abel was killed, that line continued through Seth and then Enosh. The other lineage came through Cain.

Cain's line moved in a different direction. It began building life apart from the Spirit. It kept developing outwardly, but it did not solve the corruption that had entered the human species. The line through Abel, then Seth, and then Enosh carried the awareness that something in man had gone wrong and that restoration was needed.

From that line eventually came Abraham, and from Abraham came the line that continued through Israel until Christ. But when one focuses on physical lineage rather than what actually happened to humanity, one misses the point altogether.

Physical lineage is no longer the defining mark of identity. Before the decision in the Garden, there was no individualism, no separate tribes, no competing bloodlines. Humanity functioned as a single, unified species. When death entered, people began separating into tribes and lineages, each governed by its own subjective rules, cognitive laws, and definitions. What came next changed everything.

When Yeshua went to the cross, He put that corrupted dust species to death entirely, rendering it extinct.

This was not a religious moment. It was the end of a species. One species ended. Another began: the Christ-species.

By resurrecting, He established humanity as a new creation. A new creation is not a clean record or a metaphor for moral improvement. It is an actual identity replacement, from the dust species into the self-existent Spirit. The dust species and the lineage of darkness are one and the same. They both describe a humanity still governed by external reference points rather than the Spirit. There are now only two actual lineages on earth: the lineage of darkness, those who still live by their own independent logic, and God's lineage, those who have entered the covenant of Christ.

This is why the word was given to the Gentiles, meaning all non-Jewish peoples, through the Apostle Paul and many others. It was never about physical lineage. He taught explicitly that in the new man, the Christ-species, there is neither Greek nor Jew, because Christ is all and in all. Identifying with skin color, biological family, gender, or social class is an earthly reference point, a dust mindset, that limits humanity from its true divine capacity. Yeshua Himself made this plain when He asked, "Who is my mother and my brother, but those who do the will of the Father?" Your true ancestry is no longer defined by biology. It is defined by the resurrected Spirit of Christ within you.

Christ did not come to start a religion or give people a better moral code. He came to restore what had been corrupted in the species at its source. The promise that moved through Abraham's line was never about land, family, or national blessing alone. It was always pointing toward the restoration of the human spirit.

Those who choose to live from the restored Spirit are now the Christ-species. The Holy Spirit is not an abstract force or a distant presence. It is the self-existent logic and governing nature of God, functioning within you as your new operating intelligence.

It functions as the literal operating system of your mind and heart when you enter the covenant. God gives you this Spirit to fully validate your identity, empowering you to govern reality from the inside out rather than relying on external approval.

This Holy Spirit seals you permanently. It cannot be removed, revoked, or taken away. It is the permanent mark of your new identity as the Christ-species. As Ephesians 1:13-14 states, you were sealed with the Holy Spirit of promise the moment you entered the covenant, and that Spirit is the guarantee of everything that belongs to you in Christ.

Why Many Did Not Recognize Him

By the time Yeshua came, Israel was living under Roman oppression. Because of that, many had changed their expectations of what the Messiah would do. Instead of looking for one who would restore the spirit of man, they sought one who would deliver them from political suffering and outward circumstances.

Their expectation had shifted from the inside to the outside. But the problem was never Rome. The problem was humanity's condition. Yeshua did not come to change the political order. He came to restore the governing source within man. That is why He offended so many. He did not come to meet their agenda. He came to deal with something far deeper than they were willing to face.

By that time, many people no longer read Scripture from the perspective of the priests and prophets of their ancestors. Their priorities had shifted. Their definitions had changed. They were still reading the words, but they were no longer seeing the purpose.

The Pharisees are the clearest example of this. They treated the Torah not as the natural wisdom and expression of God's Spirit, but as a rigid system of rules for gaining external validation. They turned spiritual principles into a transactional, rule-keeping system and used it to feed their own pride and desire for power. Yeshua confronted them directly on this. He told them they focused on cleaning the outside of the cup while their inward parts remained full of corruption. They had the letter but had lost the Spirit entirely.

When the Messiah came, most did not recognize Him because they were looking outward. Only a few did, because they were willing to follow the Spirit behind what He was doing rather than the expectations others had built around Him.

How the Message Became Further Distorted

After the disciples passed away, the message became even more mixed when it was taken over and shaped by Rome.

The Roman Emperor Constantine and his councils helped frame much of what is understood today. Because they did not understand the ancient

Israelite covenants and cognitive laws, they interpreted Scripture through their own logic, mixing it with concepts foreign to the original framework.

Over time, many definitions were added, altered, or misunderstood. As a result, people began reading the Bible through priorities that did not come from the Spirit that inspired it.

This distortion did not stop with Rome. Every tradition, movement, or institution that has taken the name of Christ and used it to build a system of control, performance, fear, or cultural identity has presented a distorted version of Him. Whether it was used to justify colonial conquest, enforce religious hierarchy, demand moral conformity, or bind people to cultural tradition, the result was the same: Christ was reduced from a governing reality to a religious symbol. What remains is a system built in His name but not from His Spirit.

When this understanding is lost, what remains are people who can explain doctrine but cannot demonstrate transformation. The message becomes a system of belief rather than a living government. When the governing reality of Christ is misread as religion, everything built from that misreading becomes distorted.

This is why the issue is not religious. It is a species issue. Humanity has been trying to function well while disconnected from the Spirit it actually needs. That is why so much of life has been marked by confusion, disorder, abuse, fear, domination, and broken relationships.

Christ came to make it possible again for people to live from the Spirit, think from the Spirit, and govern from the Spirit. If that is true, the evidence around us demands an explanation.

The Reason for the Chaos

If God is so powerful and Christ already came, why is the world still full of sickness, poverty, and turmoil?

The answer begins with understanding who was given charge over the earth.

When God created the world, He did not design it to run itself. He also did not intend to manage every part of it from a distance while mankind remained passive. He created man and woman to carry His breath and Spirit and to function as the ruling authorities on the earth. The earth was designed to reflect the condition of the Spirit governing it.

The chaos we see today began when man turned away from the Spirit of God within and started looking to the outside world for identity, wisdom, and validation. In doing this, mankind adopted a conditional mindset. Because man is the ruler placed within the ecosystem, the earth began reflecting what was ruling the man and woman. The earth responds to the condition of its rulers.

This is why the problem on earth has never been political, social, or environmental. The deeper issue has always been spiritual. The rulers had become corrupt, and the world under their rule began to reflect that corruption.

When Christ came, He did not come to fix the earth while leaving the species unchanged. He came to bring an end to the old, fear-driven mindset and restore the life-giving Spirit of God to humanity. Through His death, burial, resurrection, and ascension, He reestablished the way for man to live from the Spirit again. He restored the authority to heal, to establish peace, and to bring life where death had been ruling.

So why has the world not changed fully yet?

Because heaven and earth are still waiting on mankind to function in what Christ restored. God established the earth to be governed through man, and He does not violate the order He established. He has already provided the answer in Christ. The question now is whether mankind will live from that Spirit.

Many people do not realize that He has already placed His Spirit within mankind as the answer. The issue is not that God has failed to move.

The issue is that mankind has not fully awakened to what has been restored in them.

Those meant to govern the earth are still living from fear, passivity, and broken reference points. The answer is not a new political system or a social movement. The answer is a restored species.

The earth reflects its rulers. Through the cross, burial, resurrection, and ascension of Yeshua, the ruler has been restored at the source. What was lost in the Garden has been reclaimed. What the restored ruler establishes begins to reflect life again. Marriage between two restored people is no longer governed by need, fear, or external pressure. It is governed by the Spirit within each of them. That is what the rest of this book examines.

Emancipated Illustration 1: Help

She could not sleep. Her mother's voice played on a loop in her head.

He provides. He comes home. You have everything. You're just too much, Evie.

Eve lay on her side, facing the window. The roses, now on her nightstand, stood tall. Their scent filled the room.

The fan above moved the curtains, letting the city's lights dance on the ceiling. Somewhere below, a train rumbled. A siren passed and faded. The city breathed.

She lay perfectly still, careful not to disturb Adam.

She did not want to even think about speaking to him after what happened tonight. The roses. The attempt to reconnect after such a long time.

She had seen his face in the dark. He was trying. She could feel him trying. And somehow that made it worse. Because she was trying too. And neither of them could find what they were reaching for.

When it was over, she had turned away.

Now the room was still. Only the city below moved.

She stared at the city's glow through the curtain.

Do I even want to be married to Adam?

The thought arrived without warning. She did not chase it away. She just let it sit there in the dark with her.

I don't know.

That was the honest answer. She did not know anymore. And not knowing felt like the loneliest thing she had ever felt.

God, please.

For a moment, the noise of the city seemed to fade.

She reached for her phone on the nightstand. Slowly. Slowly, she put on her earbuds.

She got online and scrolled through the dozen messages her cousin had sent her earlier that day. A photo. A recipe. A quote. A meme. She pressed play on a short video.

She sat up slightly, careful not to move the mattress too much. She changed screens. She found it. Without thinking too much about it, she pressed order.

She tried to keep scrolling, but her eyes grew heavy. She settled back on her pillow.

She was asleep before she knew it. The loop had finally stopped.

Adam lay on his back listening to the trains pass. The siren. The hum of something that never stopped. He used to hate the noise when he first moved here years ago. Now it helped him sleep. But not tonight.

When she had turned away, he found the crack in the ceiling. It danced in the city's lights.

He did not know how to fix this. He had tried everything he knew how to try, and none of it had reached her.

Tonight made him question if she...

...even loved him.

He had been carrying that question for months. He had never said it out loud. Not to her. Not to anyone. He had buried it under long hours at work.

He had been staring at it when the light of her phone cut through the dark.

He closed his eyes and remained still.

In a few moments, the light went off. He knew that breathing. Deep and slow. She was *finally* asleep.

He turned back to the ceiling. Past the ceiling.

Help us.

He drifted off to sleep.

6

Chapter 6: An Emancipated Marriage

A restored person is someone who now lives from the Spirit of God within. That restoration changes not only who they are but how they operate. An emancipated marriage is rooted in the Emancipated Mindset, which means you think and direct your life using God's reasoning. It is a marriage in which both people are living from the restored Spirit of God within. The foundation of an emancipated marriage is that each person belongs to God first. Marriage is an expression of their commitment to His standard. It is not established solely between two people. It is established between two people and the Spirit that governs them both.

A Divine Ecosystem

Because of this, you are cultivating a divine ecosystem where God's presence is honored and multiplied. That presence transforms the marriage into a restored Garden of Eden. To protect it, the couple establishes clear boundaries that keep confusion, infidelity, and outside opinions out. Within this protected space, God is the environment, the life source, and the guiding logic.

A Shared Definition

An emancipated marriage requires a clear definition and a shared vision. A couple cannot establish something strong if they have never defined what they are establishing. This means the husband and wife must take time to define their marriage and become precise about the principles they prioritize.

They must also establish common definitions. When the definitions of marriage are clear, and when both people know what they do and do not do in it, there is little room for chaos and disorder. When something happens in the home, the couple can return to what they have already defined: the same vision, the same principles, the same shared understanding. This keeps the marriage from being driven by whatever emotion is strongest in the moment. A shared definition, however, is only as strong as the pillars that support it.

The Two Pillars of the Marriage

An emancipated marriage stands on two pillars: integrity and equity. Integrity means that each person remains consistent with the truth of their own spirit. They do not abandon their principles to keep the other person happy. They do not change their identity to avoid conflict or gain approval. They remain aligned with the Spirit.

Equity means that each person recognizes the other's life, dignity, and self-determination. They do not treat their spouse as someone to rule over, manage, or control. They treat their spouse according to the spiritual nature God has given them. Because of this, the marriage is not rooted in domination. It is rooted in mutual honor and shared responsibility. In this kind of marriage, decisions are not made by asking, "How do I get my way?" They are made by asking, "What protects the life of this marriage? What serves the good of the whole?" That is why equity is so important. It keeps the marriage from becoming selfish, biased, or oppressive.

Cultivating and Keeping the Marriage

An emancipated marriage is a living ecosystem. Like a garden, it must be cultivated and kept. Friendship must be tended. Romance must be nurtured. Sexual connection must be cultivated and protected.

The marriage must also be kept. It must be guarded from whatever weakens trust, disrupts peace, or brings confusion into the home. Clear agreements matter. Honest communication matters. Boundaries matter. A husband and wife are, in a real sense, placing a fence around their garden so the life inside it can keep growing. What fuels that kind of care is not obligation. It is love. But love in this framework means something specific.

Love as Equity

In an emancipated marriage, love is not something the couple is trying to get from each other. Love is equity. That means love is not just a feeling. It is the decision to honor the life of the other person and to act in ways that protect the good of the marriage. It means each person gives the other what is needed to function and thrive, rather than demanding sameness in every area.

For example, consider a husband who works from home and a wife who works outside the home. Equity does not mean splitting household tasks 50/50. It means each person gives what they are positioned to give, so the home functions well. He may carry more of the load during the day. She may carry more on the weekends. Neither is keeping score. That is love as equity. Each person contributes according to capacity, not according to a demand for identical output.

Because of this, love becomes simple and clear. If something is unfair, harmful, or biased, then it is out of line with love. If something protects life, order, trust, and peace, then it is in line with love. This gives the couple a clear way to judge what belongs in the marriage and what does not. And when love is operating this way, the natural result is peace.

Peace and Safety

In an emancipated marriage, peace and equity form the foundation of the home. Peace is not just the absence of conflict. It is the calm and safety that come from knowing the marriage is held together by clear principles and shared commitment. This kind of peace allows both people to be open and honest without fear of being mocked, shut down, or punished. It creates trustworthiness and emotional safety. It gives both people room to rest.

Peace, equity, and the kind of order this marriage needs do not hold themselves together by accident. They must be bound by something fixed. That is where covenant comes in.

Covenant

For many people, the word "covenant" already carries meaning, but it is not always the meaning used here. Same word, different definition. In this book, covenant does not mean a religious label, a duty-based bond, or a sacred agreement that binds people to disorder or control. It does not mean one person has spiritual authority over the other. It does not mean enduring dysfunction in the name of commitment. The understanding of covenant here is based on the Garden model, not on any external system.

A marriage covenant is a fixed, agreed-upon way of life directed by the Spirit of God. It begins when two self-determining people first make a personal vow of integrity to God. Because they are both joined to the same Spirit, the same vision, and the same divine logic, they can then be joined to one another. In this way, they become one in purpose and identity while remaining two distinct people.

This is how two people can become one without losing themselves. They do not stop being two distinct people, but they are yoked together by the same vision, the same commitment, and the same order. In that sense, the covenant keeps them moving together as one in the marriage, not by force, but by shared agreement before God. This can be seen in Genesis 2:24, where the two became one flesh, in Amos 3:3, which asks, "Can two walk together, except they be agreed?" and in Malachi 2:14, which calls marriage a covenant.

What It Produces

An emancipated marriage does not happen by accident. It grows when two people are willing to live from the Spirit and keep returning to the same principles that sustain life and peace. When that happens, the marriage becomes what it was always meant to be: a place where life is cultivated, protected, and multiplied. A place where both people can rest, grow, and establish life together.

What has been described in this chapter is a principled life lived between two people. Two people who have chosen to live from the Spirit, walk in integrity, and honor each other can establish something that lasts. The next chapter offers an assessment to help you identify where you are right now. Take it individually first, even if you are married, so each person can answer honestly before discussing.

7

Chapter 7: Is Your Relationship Conditional?

This assessment is meant to help you honestly examine how you think and relate, and what may be shaping your relationship. Answer each statement based on what is actually true, not on what you wish were true.

If you are married, each person should take the assessment alone first.

Use this scale:

1 = Rarely true

2 = Sometimes true

3 = Often true

4 = Very true

1. My peace rises or falls based on how loved, chosen, or wanted I feel by my partner.
2. I have mostly thought of marriage in terms of romance, safety, duty, status, or family approval.

3. Sometimes I agree to things I do not really want in my heart just to appease the other person.
4. I have stayed in an unhealthy relationship because I thought that meant I was being committed.
5. I often feel like it is my job to keep the relationship from falling apart.
6. I have struggled to maintain my peace when my partner and I disagree.
7. I have looked to a relationship to make me feel safe in a way only God can do.
8. I stay quiet, overdo things, or adjust myself too much just to keep the peace.
9. Family expectations have shaped my relationship more than I want to admit.
10. When my spouse does not tell me they love me, I do not feel loved.
11. I have believed that a hard marriage must mean the marriage is strong or real.
12. I feel unsettled when I think I am giving more than I am getting back.
13. I have expected my partner to meet emotional needs that only God can truly meet.
14. I have used silence, affection, helpfulness, sex, or distance to affect the relationship.
15. I have confused being chosen with being secure.
16. I can see signs that trust, rest, and shared order are growing between us.
17. I have looked to marriage for something I felt I was missing.
18. Religious ideas, cultural roles, or social pressure have made it hard for me to tell the truth about what is not working.
19. Instead of talking to my spouse, sometimes I go talk to a friend or family member.
20. If I am doing something for my spouse, I feel like they should do what I want.
21. When something gets out of line, we do not always come back to the same principles or definitions.
22. My confidence in the relationship rises or falls based on how my partner responds to me.

23. I can become emotionally distant when I do not feel appreciated.
24. When my spouse does not show me respect the way I want, I feel disrespected.
25. I have stayed in draining relationships because they seemed honorable, expected, or right.
26. I can become reactive when things do not go the way I hoped.
27. We are learning to root our relationship in peace rather than fear, pressure, or control.
28. I do not (or did not) like being single because it makes me feel like something is wrong with me or that I am inadequate.
29. At times, I have cared more about keeping the relationship together than about whether it was truly peaceful.
30. Our relationship is becoming more honest, more defined, and more protected.
31. I use what I do for the relationship to justify expecting things in return.
32. We do not treat God like an outsider to our marriage.
33. I avoid being emotionally honest because I do not want to feel weak, exposed, or vulnerable.
34. I can see places where fear, pressure, validation, or emotional need have shaped the relationship more than peace has.
35. When my partner becomes quiet, distant, or upset, I struggle to stay calm.
36. I sometimes think leading means making the final decision instead of building agreement.
37. I feel like when I provide, sacrifice, or carry a lot, I should get peace, closeness, or agreement in return.
38. I am growing in my ability to come back to the same principle when something gets out of order.
39. We have not clearly defined the purpose, order, and direction of our relationship.
40. My emotions shift when things do not go the way that I hoped.

Scoring

Add your total score.

40 to 69

Mostly emancipated patterns

Your relationship may still need attention in some places, but it does not appear to be strongly shaped by conditional patterns. There is already evidence of peace, honesty, shared order, and inward responsibility. Keep building on that.

70 to 109

Mixed patterns

Your relationship shows both healthy and conditional patterns. Fear, pressure, outside influence, or emotional dependence are still shaping part of it. This is where many people live without fully seeing it.

110 to 160

Strongly conditional patterns

Your relationship is likely being driven by external conditions. Fear, validation, duty, image, family pressure, emotional dependence, or performance may be shaping the way it functions. Where conditional logic takes hold, peace becomes fragile.

Reflection

As you look at your score, do not rush to shame yourself or your partner. The goal is not condemnation. The goal is clarity.

Ask yourself:

Which questions felt most true for me?

What do my answers show me about how I define marriage and relationships?

Where have I looked to relationships for peace, safety, or identity?

Where has fear shaped my expectations?

Do I see more conditional patterns or more emancipated patterns in the relationship?

What would it mean for my relationship to be built on peace instead of in conditions?

If this assessment stirred something in you, let that stirring mean something. Do not rush past it. Do not explain it away.

Do not hide behind good intentions, loyalty, or history. Tell the truth about what you saw.

Part 1 has given you language for structure, source, and spiritual logic. It has shown you that a relationship can look committed on the outside while, beneath the surface, being driven by fear, pressure, image, duty, or emotional dependence. Part 2 takes that ground and applies it. It moves from what marriage is to how it actually works, what breaks it, and how to establish it properly.

* * *

Emancipated Illustration 2: The Shift

Eve sat at the kitchen table, both hands wrapped around her mug. The early morning sun cut through the window in a single clean beam, landing directly in her cup, warming it as if on purpose. The scent of cinnamon and citrus drifted upward and dissolved into the still air around her.

She inhaled slowly.

The house held a quiet peace. In the lull of the morning, she read before heading to work. Lately, she had been getting up extra early just to sit in the morning.

The book in her hands had shifted something in her. Something she could not yet explain.

She had ordered the book a few months ago after seeing it mentioned online and had not put it down since. Not because it told her what she wanted to hear. It did not. But because the author had grasped exactly what she had been unable to name.

She had lost track of how many times she had read the little white book. She had finally stopped underlining because almost everything deserved a line under it. So she just immersed herself in its pages, moving through it slowly now, poring over each chapter as if each one were filling her soul.

She closed her eyes.

Three months ago. The dinner table. Spaghetti neither of them had touched. He had gone quiet in the way that meant the conversation was already over before it started. She had cried without making a sound.

"Do you even still want to be married, Eve?" His voice was low. Husky.

The question coming out of his mouth had shocked her, but he had finally asked her.

"I don't know," she whispered. After moments of silence, she asked, "Do you want to be married to me?"

He hesitated. "I want to be with someone who loves me."

She said nothing. She pushed her chair back, crossed the room to her work bag by the door. She set the book on the table and slid it toward him. He looked at the cover for a long moment. Then he looked at her. Then he picked it up.

That was three months ago.

She opened her eyes and sipped her tea.

Adam came into the kitchen. He moved easily, unhurried. He poured himself a cup of tea.

"Drew just called. We have to fly to the Atlanta office this morning," he said through sips. "My return flight is Sunday morning. So, I am going to check in on my mom, and we are going to catch the Hawks and Knicks game while we are there." He said, beaming.

Eve waited for Adam to finish speaking about his work trip, seeing his mother, and the game. As he spoke, she smiled, knowing that only a few months before, she would have felt rejected and unimportant if he had stayed an extra day, on top of missing their date.

He came over and sat next to her.

"I know we protect Friday evenings, Baby. And I apologize, but the new CEO called this meeting. I have to jet out of here soon to catch my flight. I am not asking you to give up this weekend's date night. Does Sunday evening work for your schedule?"

She thought about it. Not about whether the change meant something *about* her. Not about whether he was choosing something *over* her. She knew where she stood. The Spirit had already settled that. She was thinking about her Sunday evening and whether it was free.

"Sunday is great," she said, smiling. "I am available after my pilates class."

"Great. Thank you, Honey." He meant it. She went back to her book. He stayed at the table for a moment, sipping his tea, but he was comfortable. Things had shifted since that night they fought over that text message from Delilah.

He had been thinking about that night a lot lately. Not with regret, exactly. More like the way you think about a moment that splits your life into before and after. That night was one of those.

"Bring that big bat of yours tomorrow LOL." That is what the text said. It had come up on the screen while his phone was face-up on the counter. Just sitting there.

Delilah was joking. But it was not appropriate. It was an office joke about a proposal he had done well on. He had knocked it out of the park, and by the end of the day, the joke had gone too far.

He had walked into the kitchen fresh from the shower. Eve was already standing. Her voice, when it came, wailed with fury.

He had said things that night he could not take back. He knew that. Eve knew that. They had both said things. But what he remembered most was not the argument. It was the silence that followed. How they managed to sit at the table for dinner was beyond him. It had to have been the Spirit.

When she stood up from the table, his chest went cold. He was certain she was leaving. He could not move. Could not speak. He just watched. When she came back, he exhaled. Then he saw what he thought were papers. His stomach dropped again. She did not say a word. She just slid them across and looked at him.

It was not divorce papers. It was a book. Small. White. He picked it up.

He wanted to do whatever was necessary to fix things between them. He grabbed his phone and ordered his own copy of the little white book.

He had been reading it every day since, usually in the evenings after Eve had fallen asleep. Some of it had made him uncomfortable. But all of it made sense. And it answered questions he did not know he had.

What shifted for him was not a single sentence. It was more like something slowly coming into alignment. A recalibration he had not asked for and could not fully explain. Over the past three months, a new calmness had settled into him. And now, quietly, it had begun to settle into their home.

He looked at her. Her head was bent over the book, the morning light falling across her in a way that made him stop for a moment.

Without a word, he reached over and refilled her cup. She looked up, found his eyes, and kissed him. A small thing. A real thing.

He was happy.

II

Part 2: Conditional Models

Part 1 identified two conditional models that have quietly replaced the Garden design. Part 2 breaks them down. Not in theory. In real life, across real communities, real relationships, and real people.

You may recognize yourself here. That is the point.

8

Chapter 8: The Personal-Fulfillment Model

In the personal-fulfillment model, marriage is often portrayed as the answer to human loneliness and the ultimate source of personal meaning. From a young age, people are shaped by stories, movies, music, and social ideals to believe that if they find the right person, they will finally feel loved, valuable, and complete. Under this model, marriage becomes a place where another person is expected to calm your insecurities, strengthen your identity, and provide steady emotional fulfillment.

From my story at the beginning of this book, you can see that I fit well into the personal-fulfillment mindset. I was always looking for a man to rescue me. Even when I did not fully understand that was what I was doing, I was looking outside of myself for love, safety, meaning, and relief.

This is why the personal-fulfillment model is unstable. It places on another human being a role they were never created to carry. According to the Garden model, life was never meant to be generated from another person. Life was meant to flow from the Spirit of God within. As Christ said, "the kingdom of God is within you" (Luke 17:21). When marriage becomes your source, spiritual codependency begins.

Romance

In the Garden model, romance is not a random emotional event used to prove love. It is a culture deliberately established within the relationship. Romance is cultivated, protected, and maintained by mutual agreement. It grows over time because both people value it and make room for it.

I enjoy receiving fresh flowers, but when not receiving flowers means your spouse does not love you, you have left the Garden. I used to think like this. That is how subtle the shift can be. Something that should be a meaningful expression of love becomes the proof that love is present. Once that happens, romance is no longer being enjoyed.

In the personal-fulfillment model, romance is treated very differently from the Garden model. It becomes an emotional high that is used to confirm whether the relationship still feels alive. A person begins to look to romance as proof that they are loved. But when romance is used as proof of love, it becomes pressure on the other person, because one person begins to expect a feeling to do the work that only commitment, honesty, and shared agreement can do. One person begins to demand emotional energy from the other, and the relationship fills with disappointment, silent resentment, and exhaustion.

This is one reason many marriages burn out. Romance is not a spiritual law or a fixed principle that remains at the same intensity every day. It is a meaningful part of marriage, but it was never meant to serve as its foundation. When people build on a feeling rather than in a clear covenant, they often conclude that they have fallen out of love. What actually happened is that they rooted it in something that naturally rises and falls rather than in a stable governing principle.

Sexual Chemistry

In the Garden model, sexual intimacy is not just physical contact. It is the physical expression of a deeper spiritual union. It is meant to flow out of trustworthiness, covenant, safety, and shared spiritual priority. In that kind of environment, sex is not used to get something. It is the expression of what is already true between two people.

In the personal-fulfillment model, sexual chemistry is often treated as a measure of personal desirability or as a way to cure loneliness. People use sexual connection to feel wanted, chosen, or emotionally warmed. Instead of sex flowing from union, sex becomes a tool for validation.

Sexual arousal and satisfaction are also shaped by priority, which is whatever a person uses for validation. If a person depends on external conditions to feel safe, beautiful, wanted, or important, then sexual connection will often rise or fall with those conditions. If a spouse provides the exact validation a person is looking for, desire may increase quickly. But if that validation is not being provided, trust and emotional openness may weaken, and sexual connection can begin to shut down.

That is why this foundation is so unstable. If sex is being used to fill an emotional void, trust is never fully built. The connection may feel intense, but it is still fragile. When the chemistry changes, or one person no longer elicits the same emotional response, the relationship becomes vulnerable to detachment, comparison, and even infidelity. A marriage cannot stay strong if sexual chemistry carries more weight than the covenant it is meant to live within.

Identity, Feeling Chosen, and Self-Worth

In the Garden model, identity is self-existent in Yahweh. Your value does not come from being chosen. Your worth is established by your covenant with God. You enter marriage already carrying life, not trying to get life from another person.

In the personal-fulfillment model, identity often becomes tied to what marriage seems to prove. There was a time when not being chosen sent me into depression and heartbreak. I now understand that the heartbreak was the result of how strongly that person aligned with the reference points I was still using for validation.

This damages the marriage because one spouse starts watching the other too closely, needing constant signs that they are still valuable, still desired, and still enough. But no human being can hold another person's identity together, nor should they try to.

Status, Image, and Social Validation

In the Garden model, your value and identity are self-existent, established within by your covenant with God. Marriage is not a performance for an audience. It is a private functioning system.

Under the personal-fulfillment model, marriage is often treated as a status symbol, a way to show that you are successful, normal, chosen, or worthy of respect. People may use their spouse, their home, and their children to support a public image. This violates self-existence because it makes the opinions of others a reference point for your worth. It also violates equity by placing pressure on a spouse to help protect an image instead of simply living in truth.

The result is a marriage filled with anxiety, pressure, and performance. If a spouse fails to reflect the image the other person wants to project, or if life circumstances threaten that image, fear and disappointment rise quickly. The marriage can begin to feel more like image management than covenant. Instead of establishing a life together, the couple may start guarding appearances, comparing themselves to others, and carrying quiet resentment.

Security, Stability, and Provision

In the Garden model, emotional and financial stability come from living in integrity with the Spirit of God. A person becomes anchored within, drawing peace and provision from God rather than from another human being. Their peace does not come from life always going smoothly, but from the fact that their source is fixed and unmovable despite circumstances.

In the Garden, provision does not define a man's worth. A man who provides is not doing so to buy validation or control his spouse. A woman can also provide. Both husband and wife have mutual authority and work together to steward what is best for the collective. The question is not who does what.

The question is what is most logical and most equitable for the life they are building together.

Because I came from humble beginnings, I always wanted a man to financially support me. But with this understanding, I now see that is not fair. When you prioritize being with someone because of their money, you are not in a relationship with that person's heart. You are in a relationship with what their money can do for you. That is not equity.

In the personal-fulfillment model, security is often defined by the spouse's ability to calm fear, reassure, or provide financial safety. Over time, that can become exhausting. One person feels burdened and used, while the other remains chronically uneasy. What looked like closeness can slowly turn into a transactional relationship.

Shared Goals and Compatibility

In the Garden model, compatibility is not about sharing the same hobbies or lifestyle. At the deepest level, compatibility is about shared spiritual priority. Two people agree on what directs their lives, what they are establishing, and what source they live from. Their union is not held together by preferences alone, but by shared direction and covenantal vision.

In the personal-fulfillment model, shared goals are often centered on outward success. The couple may unite around buying a house, advancing a career, raising admired children, or creating a certain image. None of these things is automatically wrong. The problem is when these goals become the main glue of the marriage.

If marriage is held together mainly by outward goals, the relationship weakens when those goals are achieved, delayed, or lost. Once the project changes, the couple may realize they were functioning more like partners in a shared plan than two people joined in a covenant. They may stay together, but inwardly they have become disconnected, competitive, or emotionally distant.

Jesus said in Matthew 7:24-27 that what is rooted in the right foundation stands, and what is rooted in the wrong one falls. That principle applies here, too. A marriage rooted in external goals is still a marriage rooted in dust.

When romance, sexual chemistry, identity, status, security, and shared goals are all filtered through the personal-fulfillment model, they begin to revolve around one quiet question: What does this marriage do for me personally? That question does not always sound selfish, but the reference point is still the individual's personal fulfillment and validation. It teaches people to enter into marriage based on what another person can give them rather than on what two people can build together before God. The next chapter examines the second model, which moves in the opposite direction but arrives at the same corrupted place.

9

Chapter 9: The Family-and-Community-Governed Model

While the personal-fulfillment model treats marriage as a tool for individual emotional validation, the family-and-community-governed model moves in the opposite direction. In this model, marriage does not exist primarily for the two people in it. The two people are expected to serve the family, the culture, the religious system, or the social order around them.

This model often treats marriage as something that exists to keep order, protect reputation, fulfill expectations, and preserve the larger structure. Instead of asking whether the relationship is built on peace and equity, the focus shifts to whether the marriage is doing its job for the outside world.

In the Garden model, marriage is meant to be a living union between two people, joined in spirit, truth, and shared responsibility before God. But in the family-and-community-governed model, outside influences often become the authority. Because this model relies on external pressure to enforce compliance, it often runs counter to the original design of marriage and can turn it into a mechanism of survival, performance, and control.

Duty and Obligation

In the Garden model, duty flows from integrity. A person keeps their word because they value truth, agreement, and the life they are establishing with their spouse. Responsibility is not meaningless labor. It is the natural expression of love, order, and commitment.

In the family-and-community-governed model, duty is often an external burden. A person stays in the marriage, performs tasks, and carries responsibilities mainly because they feel they have to. The focus becomes endurance, performance, and obligation.

Family Expectation

In the Garden model, marriage forms a new ecosystem with clear boundaries. Genesis says that a man shall leave his father and mother and cleave to his wife. This means the marriage is meant to become its own Garden. The couple is not meant to be governed by outside voices, family demands, or divided loyalty.

In the family-and-community-governed model, parents, extended family, cultural traditions, and social expectations often continue to shape the marriage. Decisions about money, time, children, loyalty, and even conflict may be influenced more by the crowd than by the couple's own agreement.

When outside voices shape the marriage, the couple is no longer free to govern from within. Instead of being fully joined to one another, they remain tied to the demands of the family system around them.

Survival and Preservation of the Family System

In the Garden model, the relationship is meant to protect life, peace, and shared growth. The home serves the Garden, supporting the life within it.

In the family-and-community-governed model, the marriage is often preserved for the sake of the system itself. The goal becomes keeping the house, the name, the family line, the finances, or the public status intact. This marriage can often remain, even if the connection itself is dry, cold, unsafe, or broken.

This produces a marriage held together by external pressure rather than truth. From the outside, everything may still look stable. The family may appear respectable. The home may still function. But if the two people are no longer truly joined in heart, truth, and peace, then the structure is being preserved while the relationship is being neglected.

Status and Social Order

In the Garden model, marriage is not meant to function as a badge of respectability. Its meaning does not come from how it looks to society. Its meaning comes from the life, truth, and covenant established between two people before God.

In the family-and-community-governed model, marriage often has public significance. It can be used to signal morality, stability, maturity, family honor, or social rank. Spouses may focus more on appearances than on an authentic heart connection.

Order, Roles, and Structure

In the Garden model, roles are shaped by wisdom, agreement, and what best serves the life the couple is establishing together. The question is not whether a task belongs to the man or the woman by social expectation. The question is what is most logical, equitable, and life-giving for the whole.

In the family-and-community-governed model, roles are often assigned in advance by culture, religion, or tradition. Men may be told they must always provide, lead, and protect in a certain way. Women may be told they must always submit, serve, and function within a narrow role, regardless of wisdom, capacity, or mutual agreement.

When roles are forced instead of agreed upon, the marriage becomes lifeless. One person may feel boxed in. The other may feel burdened. Instead of working together in wisdom, the couple ends up serving a system.

Hierarchy and Authority

In the Garden model, authority is not about one person ruling over the other. It is about shared responsibility under God. Husbands and wives are meant to honor one another, protect one another, and govern the marriage in truth together.

In the family-and-community-governed model, authority is often treated as a vertical chain. One person is expected to lead, and the other is expected to follow. In many cases, the man is assumed to hold the higher place by default, while the woman is expected to yield regardless of whether there is wisdom, equity, or mutual agreement. Much of this stems from understanding Scripture through a conditional mindset rather than through the framework in which the Bible was actually written.

This is most evident in how Ephesians 5 has been taken out of context. Many people highlight verse 22, "Wives, submit yourselves unto your own husbands," while completely dismissing verse 21, "Submitting yourselves one to another in the fear of God." The Apostle Paul was teaching mutual submission and spiritual equity, not establishing a male-dominated hierarchy.

In a biblical covenant, to submit and to love mean the same thing. Spouses are not submitting to the arbitrary demands of an individual. Both partners are willingly submitting to the covenant, the mutual agreements, and definitions they established together. To lead simply means being a servant to the covenant and protecting the integrity of the relationship.

By distorting these scriptures, the conditional mindset has left many marriages in the dark, turning them into master-slave dynamics. When a husband assumes the right to rule over his wife, he can suppress her self-determination and act as an oppressor.

Domination and Control

In the Garden model, people do not force one another into agreement. They speak truth, honor freedom, and establish trust. Real connection grows in safety, honesty, and respect.

In the family-and-community-governed model, authority can become a tool for control. A spouse may use anger, fear, guilt, silence, threats, or religious language to overpower the other. In that environment, the goal becomes compliance.

This destroys intimacy. A controlled spouse may stay outwardly but withdraw inwardly. The home may still look orderly, but underneath it becomes a place of fear, exhaustion, and quiet rebellion. Control may produce compliance. But it cannot produce desire or trust.

Religious Expectation and Moral Obligation

In the Garden model, right living flows from life in the Spirit of God. A couple honors truth, love, and peace because those things are becoming real within them. Their agreement with God shapes the marriage.

In the family-and-community-governed model, religion can become a pressure system. People may use religious language, rules, or moral fear to force a person to stay in an unhealthy marriage or endure destructive treatment in the name of righteousness. Instead of helping people live in truth, religion can sometimes keep people more focused on appearances and obligation than on what is actually true.

This causes deep confusion. A person may begin to mistake suffering for holiness or pressure for obedience. They may stay in something dead because they are afraid of failing God, when in reality they are submitting to an outside system rather than learning to live from the Spirit of God.

When we look at duty, family expectation, survival of the family system, status, roles, hierarchy, control, and religious pressure, one deeper question begins to appear:

What does this marriage preserve, protect, or fulfill for the family, the culture, the religious system, or the social order around it?

That question does not always sound wrong on the surface. Sometimes it sounds honorable. Sometimes it sounds stable. Sometimes it even sounds holy. But the reference point is still outside the marriage itself. The relationship is being shaped by external structures rather than by spiritual laws.

10

Chapter 10: How These Models Show Up in Real Life

Both models look different on the surface. One is loud with emotion and personal need. The other is quiet, burdened by duty and social pressure. But when you trace both back to their root, they are the same. In both, marriage is being used to get something from outside the Spirit of God. One looks to marriage for emotional fulfillment, personal worth, and validation. The other looks to marriage for order, approval, protection, and social stability. Even though they move differently, both are still drawing life from outside rather than from within.

These models are not limited to a single type of person or community. They cross cultures, generations, income levels, and religious backgrounds. Wherever people are drawing life from outside the Spirit, one or both of these models will be present.

Descendants of Slaves

In communities shaped by slavery, such as descendants of African slaves, marriage and relationships are often influenced by fear, endurance, and the need for stability. This does not mean every person or every family is the same. It means many people in these communities inherited ways of thinking that were formed under oppression rather than equity and pass those ways of thinking down each generation.

In some cases, the family-and-community-governed model manifests as rigid role expectations, control, or a need to suppress conflict and maintain appearances at all costs. In other cases, the personal-fulfillment model shows a deep need for a relationship to provide safety, healing, or escape from financial lack. A person may not even realize they are doing this. They may simply feel that being with the right person will finally help them breathe, rest, or feel secure.

But when survival becomes the reference point, the Garden model cannot be established. When two people ground their connection in ancestral trauma, they are using that trauma as their primary reference point and source of validation. This is not just a cultural observation. There is a spiritual law that explains exactly why this happens.

As established earlier, spiritual laws operate the same way every time, just as gravity does. Whatever you use to define your identity legally becomes your master.

If you use the Spirit of Christ to define your identity, you are a member of the Christ-species. But when a person's primary reference point, even unconsciously, remains the trauma, survival patterns, and mindsets inherited from oppression, that reference point still functions as a master. This is not a condemnation. Most people did not choose this. It was passed down. But spiritual laws do not distinguish between conscious and unconscious reference points. Whatever a person roots their identity in will shape what they produce. When the reference point is bondage, the patterns it produces will reflect bondage, even in a person who has never been enslaved.

Psalm 34:18 says, "The Lord is nigh unto them that are of a broken heart; and saveth such as be of a contrite spirit." God is not distant from oppressed people. But oppression cannot be the wisdom by which a relationship, or even a community, is governed. This same dynamic of drawing identity from external sources rather than from the Spirit shows up in many other contexts. One of the most visible is the pressure of public life.

Public Image and Public-Facing Relationships

In public-facing relationships, both models often merge. The personal-fulfillment model shows up when people use the relationship to feel admired, chosen, or validated by an audience. The family-and-community-governed model emerges when the relationship is shaped by image, reputation, and public approval. In both cases, the audience becomes the authority.

This shows up across many different contexts. Celebrities and entertainers may stay in or leave relationships based on how those relationships affect their brand or public image. Politicians may preserve a marriage not because it is healthy but because it protects their electability. Pastors and ministry leaders can face enormous pressure to present a picture-perfect marriage to their congregation, even when the reality behind closed doors is broken, cold, or unsafe. Social media influencers may perform their relationships for an audience, measuring the health of the connection by likes, comments, and public perception rather than by truth and peace.

In all of these cases, the marriage is no longer being established for the two people inside it. It is being performed for the watching world. That is why so many public relationships collapse suddenly and dramatically. They were never truly protected by covenant. They were held together by image. When the image cracks, there is nothing underneath to hold the marriage together.

When status, platform, or public approval becomes the reference point, the relationship is being shaped entirely by the outside world. And the outside world shifts constantly. It cannot hold a marriage together. This pressure to perform for an audience is not limited to those in public life. It shows up in a quieter but equally powerful way in how many women have been taught to think about love and worth.

Women and the Search to Be Chosen

For many women, the personal-fulfillment model often manifests as a desire to be chosen, wanted, pursued, and emotionally reassured. From a young age, many women are taught that being loved by a man proves something about their value. Even when a woman is strong, capable, intelligent, or successful, she may still quietly hold the belief that being chosen confirms her worth.

This can also take different forms in different settings. In some environments, a woman may feel pressure to be soft, beautiful, agreeable, and desired. In other settings, she may reject those expectations and try to prove her worth through independence, money, or achievement. But if that success is still being used to answer the question of worth, the root issue remains the same: external validation.

This pattern crosses every culture and background. In many community-based societies around the world, a woman's worth is tied almost entirely to her marital status and her ability to fulfill a prescribed role within it. She may be taught from childhood that her primary purpose is to be a good wife, bear children, and serve the family structure. In those environments, remaining unmarried or leaving a marriage, regardless of how unhealthy it is, can carry deep social shame. The pressure is not just internal. It comes from the entire community around her. Whether the pressure is subtle or overt, the message is the same: your worth depends on being chosen and staying chosen.

This is why heartbreak can feel so devastating. It is not always just about losing a person. Sometimes it exposes how much identity was tied to being chosen by that person. When that happens, the loss reveals that the relationship was carrying something it was never designed to carry: the weight of a woman's entire sense of worth. Men face a different but equally heavy burden.

Men and the Pressure to Perform

For many men, these models often show up through performance. A man may be taught that his worth is tied to his ability to provide, protect, lead, succeed, or stay in control. In the family-and-community-governed model, this pressure may come from role expectations and external definitions of what a man is supposed to be. In the personal-fulfillment model, it may manifest as ego, status, money, sexual success, or a need to feel admired.

This can make marriage feel like a place where a man must constantly prove himself. He may believe that if he performs well enough, earns enough, or holds everything together, then he will finally feel secure in who he is. But when identity is rooted in performance, peace is always fragile. If the money changes, if work becomes unstable, or if the image begins to crack, then the sense of self can start to collapse with it.

This pressure also affects how men relate emotionally. Many men are taught from childhood that vulnerability is weakness. Showing emotion, asking for help, or admitting uncertainty can feel like a threat to a man's identity. As a result, they may suppress what they actually feel and seek emotional reassurance indirectly, through sex, respect, achievement, or control.

In many community-based cultures, this pressure is even more intense. A man may be raised in an honor culture where his worth, and the worth of his entire family, depends on his ability to provide, lead, and maintain control. In those environments, a man who cannot provide is seen as a failure. Weakness of any kind, financial, emotional, or relational, can bring shame not just on him but on his family name. This can drive men to stay in marriages that are not working, to dominate rather than lead, and to shut down emotionally rather than engage honestly.

When a man's identity is rooted in performance, control, and the suppression of vulnerability, the marriage becomes a place where he must manage rather than connect. His wife may never truly know him. And he may never truly know himself. That is a heavy price to pay for an identity shaped entirely by external conditions.

This is not to say provision is unimportant. It simply is not what defines a man. The Spirit of God is the source of all provision. He created everything according to what it needs to thrive. A man who is living from that Spirit carries that same responsibility. As one who cultivates the ecosystem of the marriage, he provides because the Spirit within him does the same.

How These Models Affect Mental Health, Children, and Finances

The damage does not stay between the two people. It moves through the entire home. In the personal-fulfillment model, the reference point is emotional validation, chemistry, or personal happiness. Because of that, mental health often suffers. A person's sense of identity rises and falls with unstable outside conditions, which can lead to anxiety, depression, and emotional exhaustion.

Children are rarely spared from this pattern. Instead of being guided and protected, they may be used for comfort, validation, or emotional support. This places adult weight on a child. Finances become distorted as well. Money may be driven by fear of poverty, the need for security, or the desire for status. The other model produces a different kind of damage, but the effect on the home is just as real.

The family-and-community-governed model affects the home differently, but the damage remains real. In this model, the reference point is approval from family, cultural tradition, or religious expectations. That can deeply affect mental health because people may surrender self-determination in order to keep peace with outside voices. This can trap them in silent, unhappy relationships driven by pressure rather than truth.

Children may be raised under rigid expectations and fear of punishment rather than equity and mutual understanding. Finances may also be drained by unspoken family obligations or pressure to keep others pleased, even when there has been no real agreement between the husband and wife. In that kind of environment, the family ecosystem becomes oppressive.

Both models have been named. Both have been traced through real communities, real homes, and real lives. And in every case, the root is the same. Life is being drawn from the outside. The ruler is not living from the Spirit within.

Before moving into Part 3, take the assessment that follows. It will help you identify which model has been shaping your thinking, so you can enter the next section knowing exactly where you are starting.

11

Chapter 11: What Marriage Model Is Shaping You?

This assessment is meant to help you see which marriage model has been shaping your thinking. Answer each statement based on what is actually true for you, not on what you think should be true.

If you are married, each person should take the assessment alone first.

Use this scale:

1 = Rarely true

2 = Sometimes true

3 = Often true

4 = Very true

1. I feel more settled in a relationship when I feel admired.
2. I have confused being needed with being loved.
3. I feel exposed when I am not chosen.
4. I have wanted a relationship to rescue me from something.
5. I can mistake romantic feelings for genuine love.
6. I can tie sexual closeness to whether I feel secure.
7. I care a lot about how my relationship looks to other people.
8. Comments from others can affect how I feel about a relationship.
9. I can feel pressure to keep a relationship looking good.

10. Family opinions weigh heavily on my relationship decisions.
11. I have felt that keeping the family structure mattered more than the relationship's health.
12. I have accepted unhealthy patterns because they seemed normal in my background.
13. I feel pressured to play a role rather than be honest.
14. I have tied manhood to providing or staying in control.
15. I have tied womanhood to being wanted or emotionally chosen.
16. I can confuse suffering with being committed.
17. I have seen fear shape the way I approach relationships.
18. I have stayed in a relationship longer than I should have because of fear of being alone.
19. I can see that outside pressure has shaped how I think about marriage.
20. I can see that I may have expected marriage to do what only God can do.

Scoring

Add your total score.

20 to 34

Lower model influence

These patterns may still appear from time to time, but they do not appear to be strongly shaping how you think about marriage right now.

35 to 54

Mixed model influence

Some of these patterns are still active. Parts of your view of marriage may still be shaped by outside pressure, validation, role expectations, or fear.

55 to 80

Strong model influence

Both models are likely shaping how you see marriage, love, and your own worth. That does not mean you are beyond change. It means you now know exactly where to begin.

Reflection

Ask yourself:

- Which statements felt easiest to admit?
- Which ones made me uncomfortable?
- Do I lean more toward needing validation or toward pressure from family, culture, or roles?
- Where have I looked outside of myself for worth, safety, or direction?
- What do my answers show me about how I currently view marriage?

After reflecting on your answers, you now have a clearer picture of where you are starting from. That honesty is not a setback. It is the beginning of real change. Part 3 is where the work begins. It provides practical manuals for establishing the Garden model in your marriage.

III

Part 3: The Garden Model Manual

Part 3 is a manual. Not theory. Practical instruction for establishing the Garden model in your life and your marriage. Read it carefully. Apply what you find.

12

Chapter 12: The Manual for Self-Existence

This chapter marks the beginning of the manual portion of the book. Up to this point, the book has identified broken relationship models and named the false sources people often use in marriage. From here forward, the focus is on practical function. A manual explains how something is designed to work, what is required for it to work, what interferes with that function, and how to maintain it over time. Read these next chapters that way.

Function Overview

To function within the Garden model of marriage, self-existence is required. This applies whether a person is single or already married. If a person is not self-existent, they will use marriage to get something they believe they lack. They will look to a spouse for identity, peace, reassurance, rescue, or security. That places pressure on the relationship from the beginning. The purpose of this chapter is to help the reader stop looking to another human being as a source of life and begin learning how to live from the Spirit of Christ within.

To understand the mechanics of this, consider the difference between a house powered by a portable battery and one connected to its own dedicated power grid.

A person without self-existence is like a portable battery. They have a limited supply of peace and must constantly "plug in" to their spouse to recharge their sense of worth. If the spouse is unavailable or the connection is weak, the battery drains, and the lights go out.

Self-existence is like a home that has its own internal power station. Because the Spirit of Christ is the central power source, the house does not need to drain energy from the neighbor to keep the lights on. It has a constant internal flow that keeps it bright regardless of what is happening outside.

This chapter defines self-existence, explains why it is required before marriage, and outlines how to establish and maintain it.

Technical Definition

Self-existence means that your identity, peace, and worth are no longer drawn from another person or from changing external conditions. It means the Spirit of Christ has become your Source. This does not mean isolation, emotional numbness, or pretending you do not want love and connection. It means nothing external has the authority to shape your emotions or decide your worth.

When a person is self-existent, marriage is no longer their answer to fear, emptiness, or instability. They are no longer asking a relationship to tell them who they are. They can still desire marriage, enjoy marriage, and establish a marriage, but they are not depending on it to give them life. They are coming into marriage with life already within them.

Requirements for Healthy Function

To function self-existently, a person must be willing to identify their external reference points. That may be being chosen, admired, protected, reassured, or seen as successful. They must stop making other people responsible for their thoughts about themselves. They must return to the Spirit of God as their source and accept that marriage in itself is not a healer.

A self-existent person functions differently in a relationship. They can love without clinging. They can receive affection without turning the other person into an idol. They can disagree without falling into depression. They can be honest without trying to manipulate the outcome. They remain integrous to their Spirit when their spouse's behavior shifts. They enter marriage to establish a life with another person, not to be completed by them.

Signs of Not Functioning Self-Existently

A person is not functioning self-existently when their peace quickly rises or falls with attention, affection, romance, sex, money, or approval. If someone pulls away and immediately feels panic, rejection, or a sense of worthlessness, that reaction is telling them something. If they need constant reassurance to feel okay, that is showing them something. If they confuse being chosen with being valuable, that is showing them something.

A person may also not be functioning self-existently when they feel empty if they are not admired, wanted, or affirmed. They may overreact when conditions change.

They may use romance as proof of love, or sexual intimacy as proof of safety and connection.

These signs are not meant to shame the reader. They are meant to help them see what has been a source in their lives.

Common External Sources

Most people do not realize how many outside things they have used in place of the Spirit of God. Some people use romance. Some use sex. Some use money, status, or family approval. Some use performance. Some use being needed. Some use control. Some use being chosen. Some use being admired. Some use protection. Whatever a person uses as a source of stability, value, or security will begin to shape their emotions.

Step-by-Step Operating Procedure

When a person realizes they are reacting from an outside source, they need a practical way to return.

Step 1: Identify the external validation

The first step is to stop and look at what just happened. What changed? What upset you? What made your emotions move so quickly? Stay with the facts first. Do not rush into the story you are telling yourself about the situation. Ask what unauthorized external condition just shifted and why it mattered so much.

Step 2: Identify the emotion

The next step is to determine what you are actually feeling. Is it fear, rejection, anger, shame, sadness, panic, or emptiness? Do not rush past this. If you cannot name the emotion, you will not be able to understand what is driving your reaction.

Step 3: Identify the source

Once the emotion is clear, look underneath it. Ask yourself what you were expecting from this person or situation. Were you looking for reassurance, attention, worth, safety, control, or approval? This step matters because it exposes what you were depending on.

Step 4: Return to the Spirit as your source

When you can see the external source clearly, stop making the other person responsible for fixing your emotions. Do not use blame, silence, withdrawal, pressure, or performance to get your peace back. Instead, return to the Spirit as your source.

First, confess that the Spirit of Christ, not that external thing, is your true source of validation.

Second, take a moment to acknowledge that His Spirit is the one living and breathing inside you.

Third, take the energy from that emotional reaction and use it to speak spiritual truths over yourself until your mind and emotions shift from panic to peace.

To ground yourself, you may use Psalm 91:2: "I will say of the Lord, He is my refuge and my fortress: my God; in him will I trust." In this framework, the Lord being referenced is the Spirit of Christ within you. Speak it slowly and deliberately until the truth of it settles in your spirit.

Step 5: Re-engage with the Spirit

Reestablish your identity, your peace, and your worth internally. Consciously refuse to make the other person your answer, your savior, or your source of validation. This is a decision you make.

Troubleshooting

Sometimes a person understands the truth and still feels friction. That does not mean the process failed. This is normal. Here is how to troubleshoot the most common malfunctions:

I still feel disturbed even when I know better.

Knowing the truth intellectually is not the same as having it as your internal reference point. Your mind has built deep neural pathways and habits over years of relying on external validation. When you feel disturbed, it simply means your system is trying to walk down an old, familiar path. Do not panic. Return to steps one to five. Repetition and routine will make this a norm.

I keep wanting reassurance.

If you find yourself desperately wanting reassurance, it usually means that reassurance has been your source of validation. Notice this pattern without shame or self-condemnation. Before you demand that your partner fix your emotional state, return to your Spirit to reestablish your worth internally.

I am already married and realize I have been extracting.

Do not panic, and do not fall into guilt. The fact that you are aware means you are on the right track. Acknowledge that you have been operating codependently, and begin taking full responsibility for what you have been unfairly asking from your spouse.

My spouse is still externally driven.

You cannot force another person into self-existence, nor can you force them to change their reference points. Attempting to do so violates their self-determination and will only create resistance and resentment. You must begin with yourself. Stop the old way of thinking by either begging for validation or attempting to control their reactions. Maintain your peace, and let the Spirit of Christ in you become the new baseline.

Maintenance Guidelines

To maintain a self-existent system, you must establish a daily routine. Your internal peace is maintained through consistent maintenance, not spontaneous effort. Daily maintenance includes:

- Checking what disturbed your peace and tracing it back to a false expectation.
- Noticing what you thought first when you felt empty or afraid.
- Refusing to let your fluctuating feelings become the ultimate authority

over your actions.

- Telling the truth to yourself quickly about what you are using as a source.
- Returning to your Spirit to stabilize before reacting to your partner.
- Receiving love and affection without turning it into a required proof of your worth.
- Practicing internal stability even when external circumstances or your partner's moods shift dramatically.

Application for Married and Unmarried Readers

If a person is unmarried, becoming self-existent means learning to stop looking to marriage for rescue. It means learning how to live from within before joining life with someone else.

If a person is already married, becoming self-existent means identifying where they have been asking the relationship to bear what validates them. It means learning to return to the Spirit as their source while still inside the marriage. When that happens, they stop draining the relationship and begin pouring life into it.

Summary of Use

To function self-existently and operate your relationships according to their proper design:

- The Spirit of Christ in you must be your exclusive source of life and identity.
- Your peace cannot be determined by the amount of attention you receive.
- Your worth cannot be determined by whether or not you feel chosen.
- Your emotional reactions must always be traced back to their root source.
- Marriage must no longer function as your emotional rescue plan.
- You must learn to actively pour life into the relationship, rather than extract from it.

Glossary of Terms

- **Self-existence:** Living from the Spirit of God as your primary source of identity, peace, and worth.
- **Source:** The primary entity you depend on to feel stable, valuable, or secure.
- **Reference point:** The standard you use to define yourself and guide your reactions.
- **Validation:** Using outside confirmation to establish legal standing for your identity.
- **Garden model:** God's structural design for relationships rooted in life together, agreement, and equity.
- **Agreement:** The formal mutual understanding that shapes how two people live and function together.
- **Function:** Operating according to the legal specifications of the original design.
- **External condition:** An unauthorized thing outside of you that you are using to shape your emotions.

13

Chapter 13: The Manual for Establishing the Ecosystem

Function Overview

Two self-existent people coming together is only the beginning. The environment they establish together must be established correctly. Without a clearly defined habitat and ecosystem, even two Spirit-led people can drift into confusion, vague expectations, and silent resentment. The purpose of this chapter is to help the couple understand the kind of environment marriage requires and how to intentionally establish it.

To understand the mechanics of this, consider a fish. A fish thrives in water because it breathes through gills. Remove it from that habitat and place it on dry land, and it will struggle, suffocate, and die. Not because something is wrong with the fish. Because it is in the wrong environment. Marriage works the same way. It was designed to live in a specific atmosphere and function according to specific principles. It is not just a romantic feeling or a social title. It is a habitat and a living ecosystem. If it is going to survive and thrive, it must be established with intention.

This chapter defines what a habitat and an ecosystem are, how to establish them, and what threatens them when left unattended.

Technical Definition

The habitat is the protected, authorized environment where life is meant to exist safely. The ecosystem is the functional cycle of interactions and agreements that takes place within that environment. The habitat is the structural space itself. The ecosystem is the life, order, and function that occur within that space.

In marriage, the habitat is the protected space a couple creates to house the relationship. It is what separates the marriage from the rest of the world and keeps it intact. The ecosystem is the internal operation that happens within that boundary. It includes the couple's daily routines, shared agreements, ways of speaking, ways of deciding, and ways of tending the life they are establishing together.

Requirements for Healthy Function

For the Garden's habitat and ecosystem to function well, certain things must be established from the beginning. Both people must be willing to establish it with intention. They must be willing to define the relationship clearly, rather than assume they already understand each other. They must be willing to create a structure that supports peace and safety. They must also be willing to protect what they are establishing by setting boundaries, honoring agreements, and refusing to normalize what disrupts the peace of the marriage.

A healthy marriage does not thrive when expectations are unspoken, roles are undefined, and no one has agreed on what the relationship is actually for. Life grows where the structure is clear, the atmosphere is safe, and both people are committed to tending what they have established.

What Must Be Established

To establish a healthy habitat, a couple must set shared principles, shared agreements, and clear definitions. They must define the relationship, what it is meant to protect, and how it is meant to function. They must establish clear expectations, emotional safety, financial understanding, and family boundaries. They must know what belongs inside the marriage and what does not. The structure they set in place will protect the life of whatever they establish in it. It supports it, guards it, and helps it grow.

Common Threats to the Habitat

A healthy habitat does not usually collapse all at once. More often, it is weakened slowly by seemingly small things that keep disturbing the environment. One common threat is leaving things undefined. When a couple has never clearly defined what directs the marriage, what it is meant to protect, or how it is meant to function, confusion begins filling the spaces where clear answers should have been. Another common threat is outside influence. When family, culture, social media, or others' opinions shape the relationship, the marriage loses its ability to grow as its own Garden.

Unspoken expectations are another threat to the habitat. When people quietly place demands on each other without a clear agreement, disappointment and resentment begin to grow. Over time, one or both people may start feeling pressured to meet standards that were never clearly discussed. Transactional thinking is also a threat. When love, provision, or intimacy start being measured and exchanged, the relationship begins to die. The couple can slowly begin relating to each other like opponents, keeping score instead of tending the marriage.

Step-by-Step Operating Procedure

When a couple wants to establish the Garden's habitat and ecosystem correctly, they need a practical way to do it.

Step 1: Define what directs the marriage

The first step is to clearly identify the standard that will direct the relationship. The couple must decide whether the marriage will be led by truth, agreement, and the Spirit of God, or pulled by feelings, family pressure, culture, and fear.

Step 2: Establish shared agreements

The next step is to clearly define what marriage is, what it is meant to protect, and how it is meant to function. This includes how decisions will be made, what peace looks like, how conflict will be handled, and what each person is responsible for.

Step 3: Identify outside influences

The third step is to identify the specific external forces that could threaten the habitat. These may include extended family, cultural traditions, hidden habits that weaken trust, fear, social media, and religious pressure.

Step 4: Set boundaries around the habitat

The couple must decide how they will prevent what was identified in step three from entering their space and what boundaries will keep it out.

Step 5: Create conditions that support life

The couple must intentionally create an environment marked by honesty, peace, safety, equity, agreement, and shared responsibility. To make this environment permanent, the couple must turn their agreements into predictable routines.

Troubleshooting

Sometimes a couple understands the truth and still feels tension. That does not mean the process was unsuccessful. Here is how to troubleshoot the most common problems:

One person wants the Garden, and the other still wants validation or control.

If one person is trying to stand on peace while the other is still seeking validation, rescue, or control, then the relationship is being pulled in two different directions. That will create strain. One person is trying to tend the Garden. The other is not. This requires a heartfelt conversation about what each person actually wants from the marriage and whether both are willing to establish it together.

Both people think they agree, but their definitions are different.

Sometimes, couples believe they agree when they are actually using the same words with different meanings. In that case, the conflict will continue until the definitions are clarified. The couple should once again review and update definitions.

Outside influences are interfering.

If family opinions, cultural expectations, or outside pressures keep disturbing the peace of the marriage, then the boundaries are weak. A couple cannot maintain a stable habitat if outside voices constantly shape the relationship. They must create boundaries for outside influences.

Peace disappears quickly.

If the relationship loses peace every time there is a challenge, that is a sign that the environment was not established strongly enough. A poorly established ecosystem will always create long-term problems. They will need to review and update the parameters of their habitat.

Maintenance Guidelines

To maintain the Garden's habitat and ecosystem, the couple must establish a consistent care routine. The life of a marriage is sustained through regular maintenance. Maintenance includes:

Revisiting agreements regularly to keep the relationship clear and aligned.

- Telling the truth quickly when something feels off.
- Checking for drift when old patterns, outside voices, or silent expectations begin to reenter the marriage.
- Resetting boundaries when family, culture, or other external influences begin to shape the relationship.
- Protecting peace, safety, and honest agreement within the home.
- Making sure the environment still supports the relationship rather than confusion, pressure, or performance.
- Tending to the marriage with intention instead of assuming the habitat will maintain itself.

Maintenance does not mean living in fear that something will go wrong. It means staying attentive to the life of the marriage. What is healthy must still be tended if it is going to remain healthy.

Application for Married and Unmarried Readers

If a person is unmarried, this chapter helps them understand what must be established before marriage begins to carry life. It teaches them not to enter marriage with vague hopes and undefined expectations.

If a person is already married, this chapter helps them identify what was never clearly established and what now needs to be established or reestablished.

Summary of Use

To establish the Garden's habitat and ecosystem:

- Both people must be willing to intentionally establish the environment.
- The relationship must be clearly defined, not assumed.
- Shared agreements must be in place for how the marriage will function.
- Boundaries must be set to protect what belongs inside the marriage.
- Outside influences must be identified and kept from shaping the relationship.
- The habitat must be maintained consistently, not only when there is a problem.

Glossary of Terms

- **Habitat:** The authorized and protected environment where the marriage is meant to live and function safely.
- **Ecosystem:** The internal living cycle of interaction, agreement, and life within the authorized environment.
- **Agreement:** A formal, shared understanding that determines how the

marriage will function.

- **Boundary:** A clear, defined line that protects what belongs inside the marriage from unauthorized external influence.
- **Equity:** Mutual value, mutual responsibility, and shared care for the life of the relationship.

14

Chapter 14: The Manual for Mutual Reverence and Intimacy

Function Overview

Consider how a living thing responds to the way it is handled. A plant that is watered, given light, and kept at the right temperature will grow. One that is neglected, exposed to harsh conditions, or handled carelessly will weaken, even if it started healthy. The plant does not decide to die. The environment determines what it produces.

Reverence, honor, and intimacy function the same way. They are not random feelings that arise on their own. They are the natural result of how two people choose to handle one another over time. Where there is consistent care, honesty, and safety, closeness grows. Where there is carelessness, contempt, or dishonesty, closeness weakens, regardless of how strong the original feelings were.

This chapter defines reverence, honor, and intimacy, explains how they grow in a marriage, and explains what damages them when they are not protected.

Technical Definition

Reverence is the authorized manner in which a person handles what is sacred and worthy of care. Honor is the deliberate act of recognizing the inherent value of another and responding to that value with right administration. Intimacy is the spiritual and cognitive closeness that grows as safety, honesty, and trust are established. It is not limited to sex. True intimacy includes emotional, spiritual, mental, romantic, and physical closeness. It grows where people are handled with the care required by their original design.

Requirements for Healthy Function

For this part of the Garden to function, both people must be willing to see each other truthfully and treat one another as valuable based on the sovereignty of the Spirit within them. They must be willing to speak honestly and treat each other with care. They must avoid using fear, silence, manipulation, or control to deal with tension. They must also protect trust. Trustworthiness is the consistent reliability of a person's character and actions over time. If trustworthiness is missing, intimacy will weaken no matter how strong the feelings once were.

What Must Be Established

For reverence, honor, and intimacy to grow, the environment must include several elements. Emotional safety must be established, which is a protected environment where truth can be spoken, and the Spirit can be expressed without fear of ridicule, retaliation, or manipulation. When a person feels they must constantly defend their mind, body, or emotions, the connection operates in survival mode rather than peace.

Honesty must be the norm, which means speaking the truth without using words to seek validation or approval.

Consistency must be present, meaning actions stay aligned with words and agreements over time. Without unbroken behavioral patterns, trust cannot exist, and without trust, true intimacy is impossible.

Areas of vulnerability must be handled with care. Using a person's history or emotional openness to gain an advantage or to shame them will create distance within the ecosystem.

Each person's self-determination must also be honored. Self-determination is the inherent, divine right and responsibility of an individual to direct their own voice, reasoning, and choices. A healthy connection never places a demand on another Spirit. The couple must also make it clear that manipulation, contempt, fear, and control have no place in the relationship.

Common Threats to Reverence, Honor, and Intimacy

Intimacy is slowly weakened by repeated violations, not by sudden collapses. Common threats include dishonesty, contempt, carelessness in speech, and manipulation. Intimacy is also damaged when one person keeps score, uses sex to get validation or control, or treats the marriage as something that will maintain itself without care. When these patterns persist without correction, the ecosystem weakens regardless of the strength of the original connection.

Step-by-Step Operating Procedure

The following steps give a couple a practical way to establish reverence, honor, and intimacy in the relationship.

Step 1: Learn how to handle one another

The first step is to define what kinds of treatment belong in the relationship and what do not. The couple must agree that the relationship will be handled with care, honesty, and respect.

Step 2: Establish emotional safety

The next step is to make space for truth. Both people need to know they can speak openly without being crushed for telling the truth. Honesty and care must operate together. Truth spoken without care can damage the ecosystem just as much as silence.

Step 3: Practice honor in daily interaction

Honor must be practiced. This means speaking carefully, listening without contempt, and responding without diminishing or controlling the other person. It means treating the other person's voice and views as valuable within the relationship.

Step 4: Establish trustworthiness through consistency

Trustworthiness is consistent reliability over time. This means keeping one's word, telling the truth quickly, and ensuring actions align with agreements. It is not established in a single moment. It is the accumulation of small, consistent choices made over time.

Step 5: Let intimacy grow from the life you tend together

Intimacy does not grow through pressure or performance. It grows in an environment where both people feel safe, truthful, and well cared for. As the other steps are practiced consistently, closeness will follow naturally. The couple should check in with one another periodically to assess whether the environment still feels safe and honest for both people.

Troubleshooting

Sometimes a couple understands the truth and still feels stress. That does not mean the process is faulty. Here is how to troubleshoot the most common problems in this part of the Garden.

One person is honest, and the other shuts down.

If one person stays engaged and the other keeps withdrawing, then safety is not yet strong enough. The environment still needs the steps applied or a conversation about what is taking place.

The relationship feels functional but not close.

Sometimes a couple may inwardly feel distant from one another. This usually means trust, honor, or emotional safety needs attention. Closeness is the natural result of trustworthiness, safety, and care. Revisit the steps again together.

Physical intimacy is present, but closeness is weak.

If sex is present but emotional or spiritual closeness is weak, then intimacy is not functioning as a whole. One part of the relationship is active, while another is neglected. A heartfelt conversation must take place about caring for one another's thoughts and emotions.

One person feels mishandled.

If one person feels repeatedly dismissed, controlled, or spoken to carelessly, reverence and honor may be absent. An adjustment in these areas is needed.

Maintenance Guidelines

To maintain reverence, honor, and intimacy, the couple must practice consistent care. The health of this part of the relationship is sustained through regular maintenance, not occasional effort. Maintenance includes:

- Telling the truth quickly when something feels off.
- Addressing disrespect early instead of letting it grow.
- Keeping tone, words, and actions aligned with honor.
- Revisiting agreements that help each person feel safe and handled well.
- Refusing to let resentment build in silence.
- Protecting the emotional atmosphere of the relationship.
- Tending intimacy with intention instead of assuming it will survive on its own.

Application for Married and Unmarried Readers

If unmarried, this chapter helps you understand what kind of atmosphere and treatment must exist for a relationship to be healthy. It also helps you stop confusing chemistry with true intimacy.

If married, this chapter helps you identify where reverence, honor, or trustworthiness may be weak. It gives you language for what needs strengthening so that closeness can grow again.

Summary of Use

To establish mutual reverence, honor, and intimacy:

- You must handle one another with care.
- You must make truth safe.
- You must practice honor in daily life.
- You must establish trustworthiness through consistency.
- You must allow intimacy to grow from the environment you establish, not

from pressure or performance.

- You must keep tending the relationship so that unity does not weaken.

Glossary of Terms

- **Reverence:** The authorized manner of handling something as sacred and worthy of care.
- **Honor:** The deliberate act of recognizing inherent value and responding to it with right administration.
- **Intimacy:** The spiritual and cognitive closeness that grows through honesty, safety, trust, and living together in truth.
- **Trustworthiness:** The state of consistent character and reliability over time.
- **Emotional Safety:** A protected environment where truth can be spoken without fear, ridicule, or manipulation.
- **Self-determination:** The inherent, divine right and responsibility of a person to direct their own voice, reasoning, and choices.
- **Closeness:** The natural result of trustworthiness, safety, and care.
- **Consistency:** The state of actions staying aligned with words and agreements over time.
- **Contempt:** The unauthorized act of treating another person as beneath your own status or value.
- **Vulnerability:** Open honesty without using pain to manipulate, control, or bond through dysfunction.
-

15

Chapter 15: The Manual for Spirit-to-Spirit Communication

Function Overview

Consider a garden that depends on two irrigation channels to stay alive. The soil is good. The seeds are good. Everything needed for life is already present. But if one of the channels gets blocked or diverted by careless habits, the garden does not receive what it needs. The problem is not the garden. The problem is how the water is being directed.

Communication in a marriage works the same way. The Garden is already present. The Spirit is already the source. What determines whether the marriage stays alive is how two people direct what flows between them every day. If the daily habits of speaking, listening, and responding are careless, reactive, or dishonest, the Garden does not receive what it needs to grow. If those habits are honest, responsible, and equitable, the marriage is sustained.

This chapter identifies the destructive communication habits that block the flow and gives a practical procedure for replacing them.

Technical Definition

Spirit-to-spirit communication is how two Spirit-led people speak and listen, keeping the marriage aligned with the Spirit's principles. It is directed by peace, responsibility, and honesty rather than by fear, pressure, assumption, or control. It is not simply the exchange of words. It is the daily practice of staying honest, staying clear, and staying connected to what the marriage is actually for.

In the Garden model, communication is not meant to be a tool for domination, emotional dumping, or hidden demands. It is meant to help two people stay clear, honest, and connected.

Requirements for Healthy Function

For communication to function well, both people must be willing to listen without rushing to defend themselves. Both must be willing to share openly instead of hoping to be guessed correctly. Both must be willing to practice emotional responsibility. This means taking full ownership of your mental state without making another person responsible for carrying or fixing your emotions.

Spirit-to-spirit communication also requires humility. A person must be willing to slow down, ask questions, and receive feedback. If one person only wants to be understood but never wants to understand, communication will keep breaking down. Conversation cannot be used to win arguments, punish, or control.

What Must Be Established

For Garden communication to function, several things must be established clearly. The couple must establish that both voices matter. They must establish areas to address rather than ignore. They must establish the tone and manner in which something is communicated. This is just as important as the words themselves.

They must also establish that silence will not be used as punishment, assumptions will not replace questions, and demands will not replace honest requests. If these things are not established, then the relationship will easily drift into defensiveness and continual misunderstandings.

Common Threats to Spirit-to-Spirit Communication

Common communication threats include making demands, which is the unauthorized act of placing emotional or mental pressure on another person instead of making a clear and honest request. They also include speaking over the other person, listening only to respond, making assumptions instead of asking questions, and presuming that something has been agreed upon when it has not.

Another common threat is assuming antagonism, a reactive mindset that assumes the other person is against you. Emotional dumping is also a threat, along with poor timing, careless tone, sarcasm, defensiveness, and using silence to hurt the other person.

Step-by-Step Operating Procedure

When a couple wants to establish spirit-to-spirit communication, they need a practical way to do so.

Step 1: Notice the destructive habit

The first step is to identify recurring communication patterns that harm the ecosystem. Is someone making demands? Is someone assuming instead of asking? Is someone interrupting or shutting down? Before healthier communication can be established, the old patterns have to be identified.

Step 2: Name what the habit is doing

The next step is to ask what that pattern is producing in the relationship. Is it creating confusion, pressure, fear, resentment, or defensiveness? A habit may feel normal simply because it is familiar, but that does not mean it is healthy. The couple must clearly identify what the destructive habit is producing in the relationship.

Step 3: Replace the habit with a better action

Once the destructive habit is identified, it must be deliberately replaced. A demand should be replaced with a sincere and gentle request. A presumption should be replaced with a question. Listening only to respond should be replaced with listening for understanding. Unspoken expectations should be replaced with direct communication. Assuming antagonism should be replaced with verifying intention before reacting.

Step 4: Speak from the truth of their heart

Communication in the Garden requires honesty. A person can be honest without being harsh. They can be direct without being controlling.

Step 5: Stay with the agreement

After the heart has been expressed, the couple must return to what protects the ecosystem and helps the relationship stay aligned with the Spirit. If the goal becomes winning, communication will quickly stop functioning.

Troubleshooting

Sometimes a couple understands the truth and still feels opposition. Here is how to troubleshoot the most common problems in spirit-to-spirit communication.

One person talks, and the other shuts down.

If one person keeps speaking while the other keeps withdrawing, then they may not feel prepared to speak about the topic. The goal is not to force a quick resolution. The goal is to create enough safety for both people to remain present.

The same argument keeps repeating.

Repeated conflict usually means the real issue has not yet been clearly defined, or one of the destructive habits is still active. The couple must stop treating the recurring argument as a new problem and identify the underlying pattern.

One person feels overwhelmed.

Sometimes one person talks too much, explains too much, or presses too hard for an answer. When that happens, the other person may feel overwhelmed rather than understood. The solution is to slow down and be patient.

Outside stress continues to shape the home's tone.

If stress from work, family, money, or other areas keeps intruding on the marriage, the couple must learn to recognize when outside pressure affects how they speak and respond to one another. They must understand that what is outside the marriage is secondary to the ecosystem itself.

Maintenance Guidelines

To maintain Spirit-to-spirit communication, the couple must establish daily patterns that shape the life of the marriage. Spirit-led communication is maintained through consistent care, not occasional effort. Maintenance includes:

Telling the truth quickly instead of letting confusion grow.

- Replacing demands with sincere requests.
- Asking questions instead of making assumptions.
- Listening to understand rather than to respond.
- Correcting careless tones.
- Refusing to let resentment build in silence.
- Addressing tension before it takes root.
- Returning to the agreement instead of trying to win an argument.

Application for Married and Unmarried Readers

If unmarried, this chapter helps the reader understand what kind of communication is required for a healthy marriage to function. It also helps them recognize destructive habits early, so they do not confuse chemistry with the ability to live in peace together.

If married, this chapter helps the reader identify which patterns are already shaping the relationship's daily life. It helps them stop excusing destructive habits as personality and begin replacing them with habits that support peace.

Summary of Use

To establish spirit-to-spirit communication:

- You must notice destructive habits clearly.
- You must be honest about what those habits are producing.
- You must replace demands, assumptions, and pressure with direct questions and sincere requests.
- You must speak from peace instead of emotional force.
- You must stay with the agreement instead of trying to win.
- You must maintain these habits consistently if peace is going to remain.

Glossary of Terms

- **Communication:** The exchange of honest meaning and understanding between two Spirit-led people, directed by peace rather than external pressure.
- **Daily function:** The repeated relational patterns and interfaces that shape the life of a marriage.
- **Demand:** Unauthorized emotional or mental pressure placed on another person instead of a clear and honest request.
- **Request:** A heartfelt expression of desire that respects the other person's self-determination and leaves room for their response.
- **Assumption:** The act of deciding what something means without first asking the source directly.
- **Presumption:** Moving as though an agreement has been established when it has not.
- **Antagonism:** The reactive mindset of assuming the other person is operating against you.
- **Agreement:** A formal shared understanding that protects the peace and direction of the relationship.
- **Emotional responsibility:** The act of owning your internal state without making another person responsible for your emotions.
- **Tone:** The emotional frequency and manner in which something is communicated, which determines how it is received.

16

Chapter 16: Returning to the Garden

To the one tending the Garden,

You made it.

Not just through the pages, but through the honesty this book required of you. You sat with a framework that asked you to examine your conditioning, identify the model that shaped you, and consider what it has produced in your marriage. That is not easy. Most people never do it. You did.

What you now hold is not just information. It is a different way of seeing. You understand what marriage is for, what it requires, and what has been working against it, in the culture, in the models you inherited, and possibly in yourself. That understanding is not small. It is the beginning of something real.

The principles do not change. The Spirit is the same Spirit in every person who receives Him. The same source produces the same fruit. Where the principles are applied consistently, the same Garden grows. Self-existence. A clearly established habitat. A living ecosystem. Reverence, honor, and intimacy. Peaceful communication. These are the conditions under which the Garden thrives.

The Garden model is not a fantasy. It is the restored pattern made available through the death, burial, resurrection, and ascension of Christ. He reestablished the way back. Because of Him, this is not a theory. It is a real and accessible way of living, if you are willing to take it seriously. You now know what each of those things means and how to establish them. What you do with that is yours to decide.

This book is not the end of the learning. It is the beginning of functioning as the Spirit of Christ in you, in your marriage, in your home, in the life you are tending together. The principles here go deeper than any single reading can take you. Return to it. Let it be a reference, not just a read.

Marriage is not hard. Operating from the wrong model, the wrong source, and the wrong definition of what marriage is for is what made it hard. Now you know what it actually is.

Eve and Adam found their way back to each other. It started with a little book slid across a table. It started with honesty. It started with one person deciding the marriage was worth tending. That same way is open to you.

The Garden is yours to tend. Tend it well.

In peace and equity,

-The Emancipator

A Final Word

I want to end by honoring the lineage behind this book.

I am deeply grateful to Zane Pierre and to his many years of investment in my life. His support, counsel, teaching, and continual development have helped shape how I now see Scripture, life, marriage, and myself. I write this book in my own voice and from my own assignment, but I do not write as though I arrived here alone. I am thankful for the time, patience, and precision he has poured into helping me grow in this understanding.

This book also stands within the larger research work of the International Institute of Pneumatology (IIP). IIP is a leading research institution in the Cognitive Science of the Bible. Its research approaches Scripture as a functional system for human thought, speech, and action, and it works to establish the Name of Christ for all mankind. Its work integrates biblical study with cognitive science, linguistics, and systems thinking to make these principles clear, practical, and reproducible in everyday life.

IIP's research treats the Bible as more than a sacred text. It approaches Scripture as a manual of the Spirit, a covenant charter, and a record of spiritual mechanics that can be understood and applied. Its focus is not only on interpretation but also on its practical function. It is about helping people live, think, speak, and function in measurable ways, directed by the reasoning of the Spirit.

While studying at the IIP, I founded the Emancipation Center. This book is not the end. It is part of a larger body of study, training, and application. Visit the website to learn more about Applied Life Logic and to go further.

Emancipation Center Website: https://theemancipationcenter.com

About the Author

Kourtney King is a teacher, writer, performing artist, and founder of the Emancipation Center. She also serves as the Ambassador for the International Institute of Pneumatology. Through her writing, teaching, and performance, she helps people understand marriage, identity, and life through the Emancipated Mindset in a way that is clear, practical, and applicable to real life.

You can connect with me on:

- https://theemancipationcenter.com

www.ingramcontent.com/pod-product-compliance
Lightning Source LLC
LaVergne TN
LVHW010840120826
845149LV00017B/3325

9798993162119